Windows to Imagination

Windows to Imagination

—☯—

Coloring Your Way to Stress Relief and Meditation

A coloring book for easing your mind and expanding your horizons
Includes special color journal pages

Barbara Jacobs
Artist, Color consultant, Designer, Teacher, and Author

ISBN-13: 9781533088871
ISBN-10: 153308887X

Acknowledgements

Thank you…

To the lights of my life, my wonderful children and their families; to my parents, grandparents and ancestors, and siblings; to good friends, and to life transitions.

With gratitude for a lifetime of living among the beautiful and inspiring art work created by my father, William Saltzman, who provided me with years of opportunities to keep him company in his studio and encouraged me, even as a child, to explore in many media.

Most immediately, a special acknowledgement to my grandson Marcus Jacobs, age 8 (at this time), who was my personal companion in drawing throughout the entire process as we each worked on our own projects simultaneously.

With appreciation for Thich Nhat Hanh, for his direct, inspiring and accessible approach to meditation in *Peace is Every Step, The Path of Mindfulness in Everyday Life.*

Once upon a time, in a land far, far away…

—from many folk tales

Contents

The time you enjoy wasting is not wasted time.

— Bertrand Russell

Why this Book?

- **The inspiration**
- **How to enjoy getting into coloring and meditation**
- **About the images and the** *Color Journal Pages*

How will you feel when you release the Busy-Ness of daily life and journey into a freer, more relaxed state of mind and body?

The Power of Color is all around us.

"Environmental color" is a known factor in our lives, from helping with healing to enjoying our homes more. Color is also well known as an effective way to reduce stress, and one that also allows you to be more creative in all your endeavors. Using Color – specifically *"color-ing"* of patterns and images – will help you do that for yourself.

I've always been a "doodler." How about you?

Do you remember the feeling, as a child, laying on your stomach on the floor with coloring book and crayons, being totally absorbed in the process? Like many children (and maybe even you), from a very young age I enjoyed the dreamy, "other-worldly" feeling that comes in the process of putting pencil, crayon, chalk, paint…to paper or, in fact, any available surfaces—both "approved," and otherwise.

But as we get older and become molded into rules, direction, and plans, we easily forget about this simple, instinctive pleasure. We may have even been reprimanded for doing it. In spite of that, some of us have continued to doodle and dream and intentionally make "official" art. Others of us have just enjoyed it when we can—and often have not even been aware we're doing so!

Now you have a way to open your own *Windows to Imagination* and jump right in to another, "Other-Worldly" experience that is intended to offer you an inward-focused, meditative, stress-relieving creative outlet to just simply explore the world of using color and shape in *Your own Way,* using the images I've provided here as the starting point.

More than just a "coloring book…"

Yes, this is a coloring book. There is also text. Why? Because in addition to being an artist myself, my own professional focus of the past 30 years has been to help all types of people create their living and working spaces for a more healthy environment while expressing their own inner personalities, their life/work goals, and their lifestyle preferences. I've done this work using an artistic approach to design that considers color, specifically, as a tool to create the healthiest possible living and working environments for our human needs—our emotional, psychological, and physical spaces and bodies. During these years as an architectural color consultant, I've encountered many people who feel overwhelmed and intimidated by the thousands of colors that are available to them to choose from in paint and other building and decorating materials. I have enjoyed helping these clients achieve their desired results by providing a clear path through that maze.

Since there are also many colors and materials available to use for a coloring book, the array—while exciting and stimulating—can also be intimidating. Many who would love to just jump into coloring are often stalled before they start. I empathize with their experience. So, to help clear your path through color, I wanted to start with information about color mixing, color meanings, and techniques for application. I've included sections on using color, and a "Color Associations Quiz" about the meanings of colors (with answers). I've also included a section with tips for mixing colors and choosing the best materials to use with this book, as well as some tips to help you express your own moods for the images that you communicate through color.

Coloring and Meditation
Where does the "peaceful mind" come from?

Why do we say that "coloring" is a form of meditation?
You've probably heard the expression "being in the zone…" that refers to a state of being so involved in a particular activity or process, and having an elevated state of focus, that you might actually tune out other sounds and smells that surround you. The process of "coloring" works that way also. Any creative process offers an opportunity to transcend your daily worries, become more relaxed, and contribute to your ability for better focus. These are all skills that are relevant in other areas of your life also.

You don't need a lot of experience in purposeful meditating, and "meditation" takes many forms. But there are a few easy things you can do to help with your stress relief experience.

1. **Breathe**

   Yes, it does sound simple. Yes, it *IS* simple! But to have "intentional breathing" actually be effective, we have to consciously *remember* to do it and to make it a systematic activity until it becomes automatic. So, for purposes of what we can call "the coloring experience," I recommend just sitting in a comfortable, upright position for a few minutes. You can close your eyes or just keep them soft and unfocused. Breathe in slowly for a count of six while you picture that you are an open vessel that the breath will enter and fill. Focus on the "In." At the fullest peak of in-breath, hold it lightly (not tightly) for a second or two. Then breathe out slowly until empty, focusing on the "Out." Picture your vessel becoming empty. Repeat a few times until you feel more "still."

2. **Gaze**

   With your materials in front of you, select the image you want to work on. Keeping your eyes "soft," just continue to breathe the same way while you gaze at the image. During this time, be open to any feelings that come *through* you. This will help you get into the right state of mind to make the most of your color application experience.

3. **The key: Play**

   Just start to work (*play*) with your colors and the image, and try to not over think what you are doing. The more you start to get into it, the better things will just flow. Don't even think about your breath now, just let go of everything else and it will even out as you work.

When you start your coloring, feel free to play any kind of music you like, or none at all. Focus into the coloring groove that has the benefit of creating a peaceful inner environment.

About the Images and the Color Journal Pages

About the drawn images: Hands are the key to expression

Hands are often the key—for creating, for being expressive in language, and as a more abstract metaphor for being human. These images came to me in a very relaxed, organic way. As they started to come together, the themes evolved.

About the patterns: Outside the box

The rhythmic occurrence in patterns can be intriguing once you get into it. Walking on the beach or seeing drifts of snow and leaves on the trees are examples that you can observe in nature. In the patterns here, you can explore the interconnections of the drawn spaces and shapes that, while they may seem identical at first glance, actually change. In your own coloring process you can be as detailed or as 'broad-stroked' as you are inclined to do. Using shading, color block, and pointed highlights of bright or dark colors will help you create your own meaning in the patterns. Feel free to add lines and shapes to the images and open spaces, connecting the pattern shapes to each other and even disregarding the lines entirely if that suits you. Go "outside the box."

The Color Journal Pages

Following each image, you will see a page for your own notes and drawings and a special *Color Journal Page* that includes a short form you can use as you wish to record your favorite colors. This is one way you can create your own personal color palette that will be interesting for you to track as you move through the book. You may even see a story evolving through the images, and I invite you to write your interpretations in the *Color Journal Pages*, on the pages for *Your Notes and Drawings*, or elsewhere throughout the book.

But most importantly, I hope you enjoy the process, the adventure, and the results of using your own colors, *Coloring Your Way!*

—m—

Players are artists who create their own reality within the game.

—Shigeru Miyamoto

Tips for Coloring - Jump Right In!

Anyone can use color. But in starting a new coloring book picture, sometimes the many areas of the image and the vast array of colors and materials that are available can be intimidating. The color wheel on the back cover is a reference for seeing how the colors relate to each other as they go through the spectrum. You've probably heard the terms "primary" and "secondary" colors. There are also more complex levels that evolve with blending.

Just a little bit of color-mixing information

The color spectrum is a rainbow, what you see when light transits through a prism. In painting (coloring), we can refer to the color wheel, seen as three "primary colors," which are Blue, Yellow, and Red. But how do they relate to each other as we use them ourselves? Where does Orange come in, and then Purple, or Green? These are called "secondary colors" and in mixing paints or other media they result from combining the "primaries," in various proportions that evolve from one color to another, through the spectrum. Further color developments happen in mixing colors in various proportions.

For example, let's try a simple experiment by moving Yellow (primary) towards and through Orange (secondary), and into Red (another primary)

These color shifts are all about proportion. Yellow changes to orange by adding a bit of red, so it becomes orange-yellow, then as you add more red it becomes yellow-orange, then orange (secondary), then orange-red, then red-orange, then red. By the time you've added so much red to the yellow, it's become close to 100% red with little-to-no-yellow "undertones." This color evolution depends on the amount of red that is added to the yellow.

You can use that same process by layering pencil strokes right on the drawing, or mixing water based paints in a separate small container or on a sheet of freezer paper.

Using colored pencils or types of crayons – quick tips for shading, deepening, blending, and intensifying your colors.

Combine image areas into a single color or even versions of one color, creating light and dark shades—and dimensional shapes—by applying your color over the same area to deepen the color. You don't even have to press hard or go to a darker color pencil. To create the appearance of more three-dimensional volume in a shape, start with the deeper shades at the bottom or at one side, and work toward the lighter shades at the top or other edge. That's one reason to start with a soft under-layer of color over the entire shape, and deepen it as you like. Layering is the key. A few techniques are below.

Hatch – Layering closely-spaced lines in different directions is called "Cross-Hatching" because the lines cross each other. With a soft hold on your pencil, make rhythmic, evenly spaced strokes at an angle to the paper. If your paper is textured, going in the direction of the texture will fill it and crossing the texture will put color on the high spots, leaving the lower part uncolored. Make the lines angled, and with each layer rotate the angle slightly to fill in the area in the depth and intensity of color you desire. A variety of shading, this technique does allow for pencil lines to show. You can control the depth and intensity by the amount of lines you use, which does not have to be even overall. With the right pressure, and practice, you can become adept at this technique.

Smooth-Shading Shapes – Hold your pencil softly at an angle that is almost horizontal and press very lightly. I like to use soft strokes in a diagonal direction to lay down the color that will and not show visible marks. In subsequent layers, change direction of your strokes slightly for a richer depth of color even, if it's a light color. Unlike the "hatching" technique, this method shows no visible texture or lines.

Deep layered color – Starting with a light application and using lighter colors, you will create a soft color base that you can build upon. Darker colors are more dense, more opaque. Add richness to your coloring by doubling up on color layers. Try it both ways – light over dark, dark over light – to see the varied effects.

Dense and Intense – A firm, almost vertical hold combined with more pressure will make the color very dense. You can still layer color.

Color mixing example – Perhaps you're trying to achieve a particular shade or tint of green. You might start with a yellow, then add blue…but find it's not quite "right." Maybe, then, you try layering some light strokes of orange or purple over it. This is especially effective when you're working with colored pencils, and is one reason you don't need a large number of different colors. Try some combinations and see what happens. Use the "Color Journal" pages to record your process and results.

Mixing and recording.
Use the journal pages after each image to tell your own stories in line and color.
You'll find on each of the blank color journal pages a few lines to record your color mixing and notes for each image, and the space to do your own drawing or story-telling. Doodle, add pictures, write a few statements or even a story, and record your favorite colors, coloring blends, and materials as a reference for your next coloring projects.

Choosing your favorite materials
Colored pencils, felt-tip markers, gel pens, watercolor paints (including "watercolor pencils") and gouache (an opaque, flat finish watercolor paint) are the most popular materials for coloring. Colored pencils are the most flexible because they can be applied in thick or thin lines, light or dark strokes and shading, and can even be layered for beautiful nuanced color and textural effects. You can even draw your own embellishments in the printed pages, since many of the drawings have open space to do that. Markers and gel pens are more opaque but if the points are fine enough they are great for adding a punch, especially if you want to go with the metallic versions. Watercolors and gouache are harder to use and require a special kind of paper to get the best results. In any case, you may want to insert a blank white page under the image you are working on, to protect the following pages in the book from any bleed-through of your media.

—〰—

Barbara Jacobs

*Try to be a rainbow in
someone's cloud.*

—*Maya Angelou*

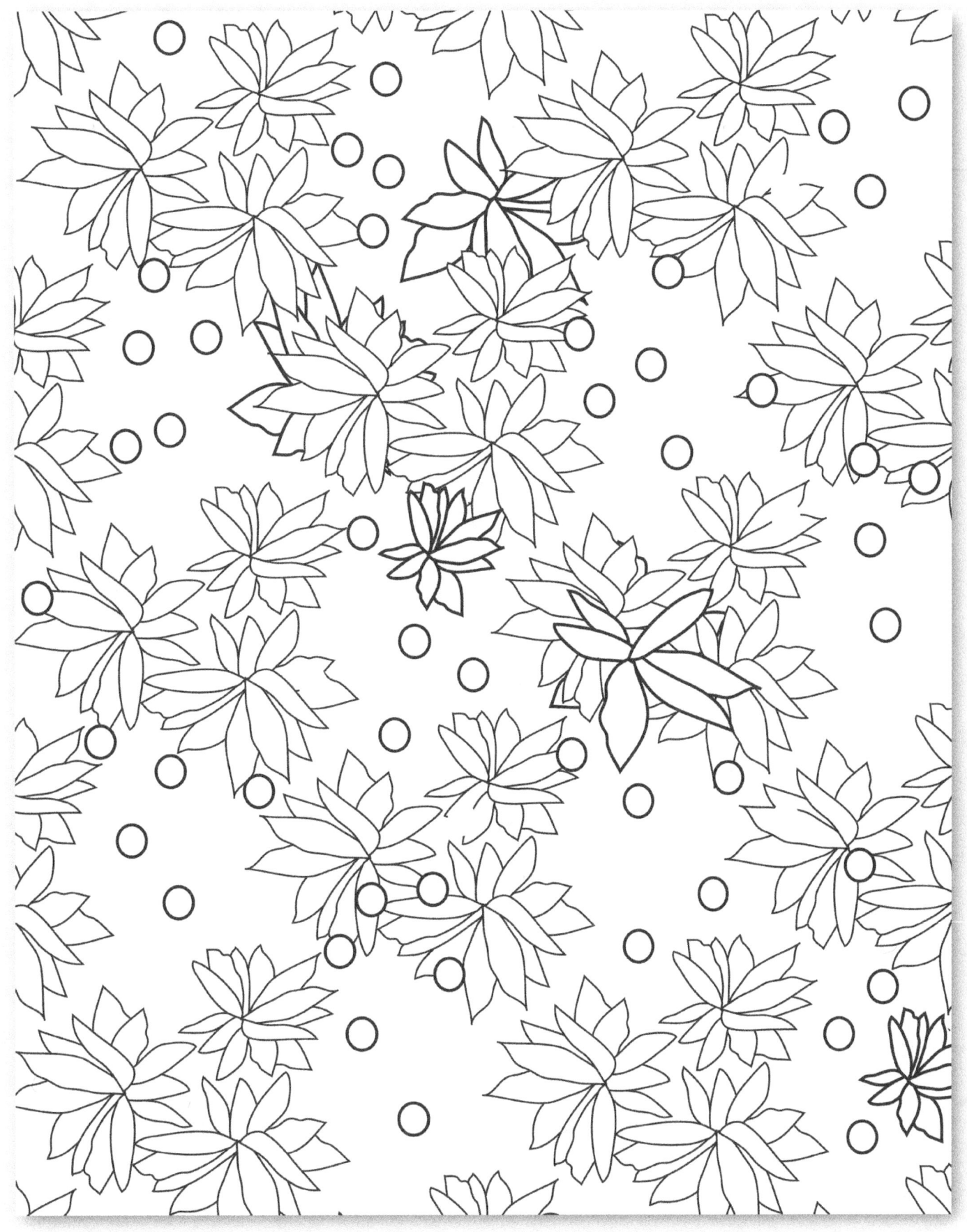

Barbara Jacobs

Your Notes and Drawings

Your Notes and Drawings

Color Journal Page

This page is a way for you to keep track of any favorite colors or color "blends."
Enjoy using this extra space for your own drawings, notes, or stories.
Feel free to use the spaces for actual colors, not just words.

<u>Love this color</u>   <u>Mixed with this color</u>   <u>Result is this color</u>

Used on this page_____

Used these materials_____

What I love about this color or combination of colors_____

Makes me feel_____

Barbara Jacobs

Color is the place where the brain and the universe meet.

—Paul Klee

What are the Windows about?

The purpose of the drawings and designs in *Windows to Imagination* is to offer you a relaxing, meditative process designed to help with relieving stress. In the pages, I've combined the drawings with a new way of looking and seeing. The drawings are defined into two very different artistic directions because, while they all serve as "Windows," the styles and subjects are different. But whether the image is simple or complex, each is created to offer you a similar process even through the different artistic styles.

Part 1 – Fantastical Voyages (the Hands series)
Hands mean so much, both literally and metaphorically. They symbolize creating, giving, caring, expressing, taking, and of course being Human! That's why they play a big part in this series.

To make your color exploration even more interesting, I've included a duplicate of each image in this group—with the second being the reverse of the first. Read the next introductory section about "Looking, Seeing, and Imagining" to find out why they are there.

Some of the images are denser and others leave more open space. Use your own embellishments and imagery wherever you like. Make it your own style.

Enjoy your adventure!

Part 2 – Patterns to Calm your Busy Life
Abstract patterns can bring you into a methodical process that allows your mind to take a break from active "thinking." You can become immersed in color in a completely creative and expressive way—*Your Way.*

Among the types of pattern design you'll see geometric, floral-based, and organic forms. Some are linear, some symmetrical, and some are more random. Some appear to be symmetrical but actually are not so, and in that may require a more detailed exploration of the shapes and how they relate to each other. I encourage you to personalize each one – "outside the lines"– to create your own new shapes.

The *Color Journal* Pages – Why, and How, to Use Them
After each image you'll see a page with space to record your favorite colors and color mixes. I've included these for you to create your own expressions. For example, you might want to draw your own pictures or write a story from a few short notes to a few pages. Some people even like to name the colors with a personal twist, like the name a friend of mine gave to a favorite color, that she calls "Power Red."

Record your favorite colors and explore your own inspired drawings in these pages and in any blank space in the book. Express your ideas in images and words. Tell your own "stories." Make it *Your* book.

These *Color Journal* pages are here as a place for your exploration and imagination to blossom, with the visual "cues" in the form of images as a starting point. Is there a story that the image—even one of the abstract or geometric patterns—brings to mind? The individual pictures are intended to provide a focus—a way to go deeper into the lines on the paper and, in doing this, get much more out of the experience.

A Note about the "Quotes"
Throughout the book I've included statements by a wide variety of people that express experiences, inspirations and sentiments that are serious, or humorous, and thought-provoking. I hope you'll enjoy using these as additional inspirations for your coloring. Embellish each of the quotes as they inspire you to decorate the page with your own color work, images, and notes. These are offered as another way to stimulate your imagination and experience the stress-relieving qualities of creative coloring.

The quotes in this book are gleaned from various sources; from online "quotes" sources to the wonderful design book, *The Art of Looking Sideways*, by the acclaimed graphic designer Alan Fletcher.

See the section on **Coloring Tips** *for more information on color use and color mixing.*

Don't feel like reading?
Just jump right in and "Color!"

—⋙—

The artist is a receptacle for emotions that come from all over the place: from the sky, from the earth, from a scrap of paper, from a passing shape, from a spider's web.

—Pablo Picasso

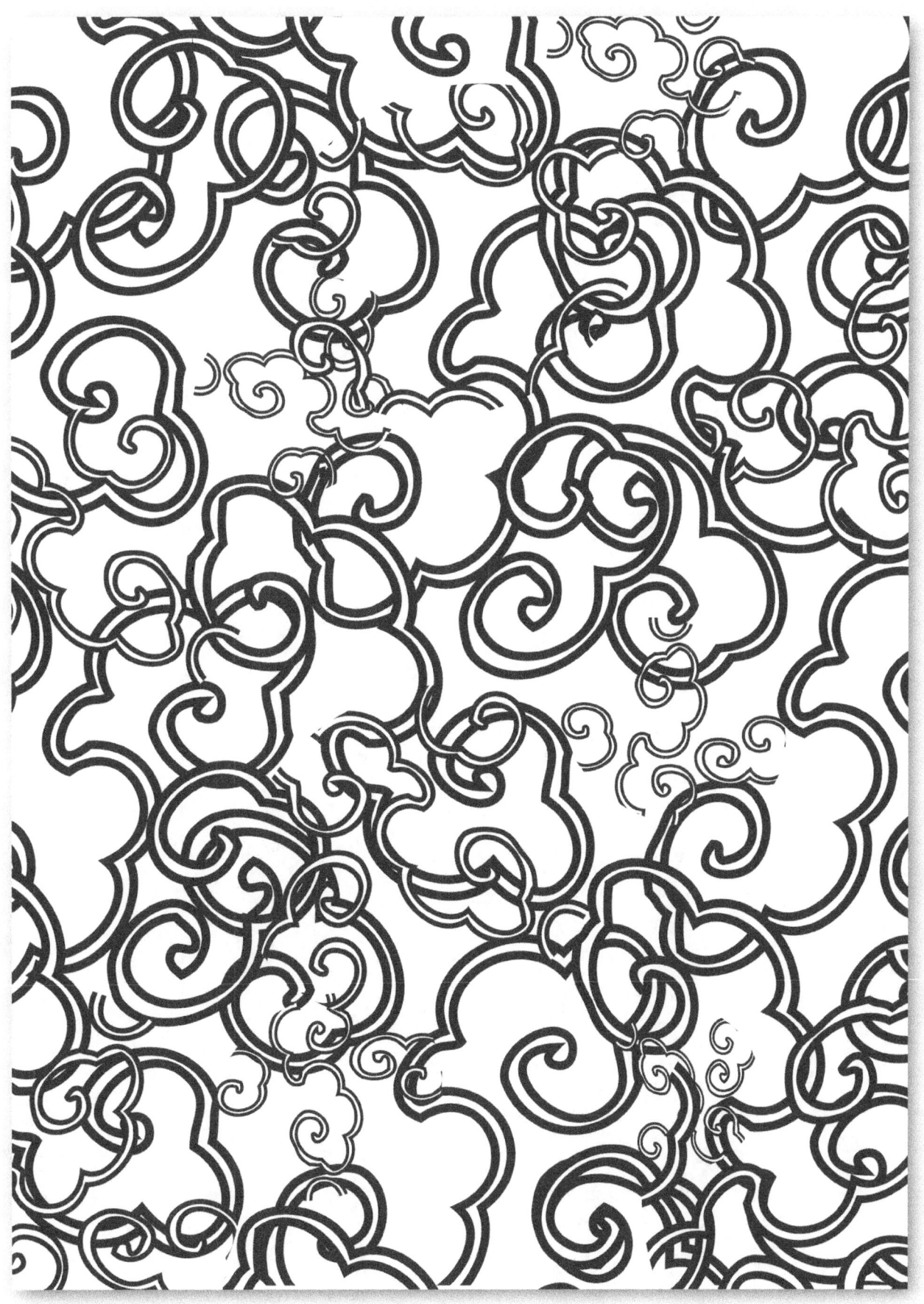

Barbara Jacobs

Your Notes and Drawings

Color Journal Page

This page is a way for you to keep track of any favorite colors or color "blends."
Enjoy using this extra space for your own drawings, notes, or stories.
Feel free to use the spaces for actual colors, not just words.

<u>Love this color</u>   <u>Mixed with this color</u>   <u>Result is this color</u>

Used on this page_____

Used these materials_____

What I love about this color or combination of colors_____

Makes me feel_____

A painter's job is to invent new ways that form can be looked at, to organize things in a way so that people notice things they didn't before. It's about letting your mind go somewhere new. Hopefully, what paintings do is give you an opportunity to inhabit another part of yourself and to see the world in a new light.

—Julian Schnabel

How to get the most from the art in this book

About Looking, Seeing, and Imagining

When looking at a book, we usually view it "right side up," and in English the spine is usually on the left side, so we turn front to back, one page to the next, in the same direction.

With ***Windows to Imagination*** I invite you to apply different ways of looking and seeing. While each image was drawn the way you see it as presented first, this is only the beginning. Actually *it does not even have to be Your beginning*!

This is what happens

When we look at anything—in print, in nature, in person—we are in a way "imprinted" by what we see as the only, or 'right' way to view it. But ***Windows to Imagination*** invites you to experience new ways of seeing, and even new ways of looking at your daily world.

Just try this

Take some time relaxing your eyes—or, as is sometimes described, "make your eyes soft" so you are not focusing on anything in particular. What usually happens is that new images start to form. Tree branches become roots…a sun image becomes rays coming up from the earth…shapes spilling from a hand reverse direction and are being gathered up…and other similar changes. Common shapes become unidentifiable in the same way.

Before you pick up your first color, take a nice long look at the image. You may see a lot of things happening, even if they are a bit abstract. Shapes will seem to connect to each other in different ways, if you are open to seeing it. Don't try too hard.

We're accustomed to seeing what artists refer to as the "positive space image." That's the part that, in a representational work, is most easily recognized as the object—or a portion of the object. But there is another equally important, intriguing piece of the art work that we call "negative space," which refers to the areas "between" the most recognizable shapes.

Try this on yourself: hold up and open your hand, spreading your fingers apart to create space between them. What do you see? Your actual fingers, most likely. But now look again, focusing on the spaces between, or even beyond, the fingers. You'll see another set of shapes entirely. Try this with anything you look at–even ordinary objects like chairs, tables, people gathering together, and objects in nature.

Then, try the process by looking at the picture "sideways," in both directions. This new way of viewing will put a completely different spin on *your seeing, your interpretation, and your inspiration.*

To provide another way to look at things in this collection of drawings, I've included a duplicate page of each of the images within the "Fantastical Voyages" section, offering you a way to have this experience with each of those drawings. This gives you a chance to try your coloring inspirations by imagining new shapes, forms, and ways to use colors.

As you start to color the various pictures...

...just take a few minutes from time to time to rotate the book by a quarter-turn in each direction, to view it sideways or upside down from the original orientation.

You'll also notice that some of the designs are more filled in while others have more open space. I invite you to add your own embellishments, designs, and even written statements on the image page or within the image itself. Feel free to go outside the lines. As I mentioned earlier, there is really no "right way." Just *YOUR* way.

Thanks for joining the exploration.

—ɯ—

Barbara Jacobs

The job of the artist is always to deepen the mystery.

—*Francis Bacon*

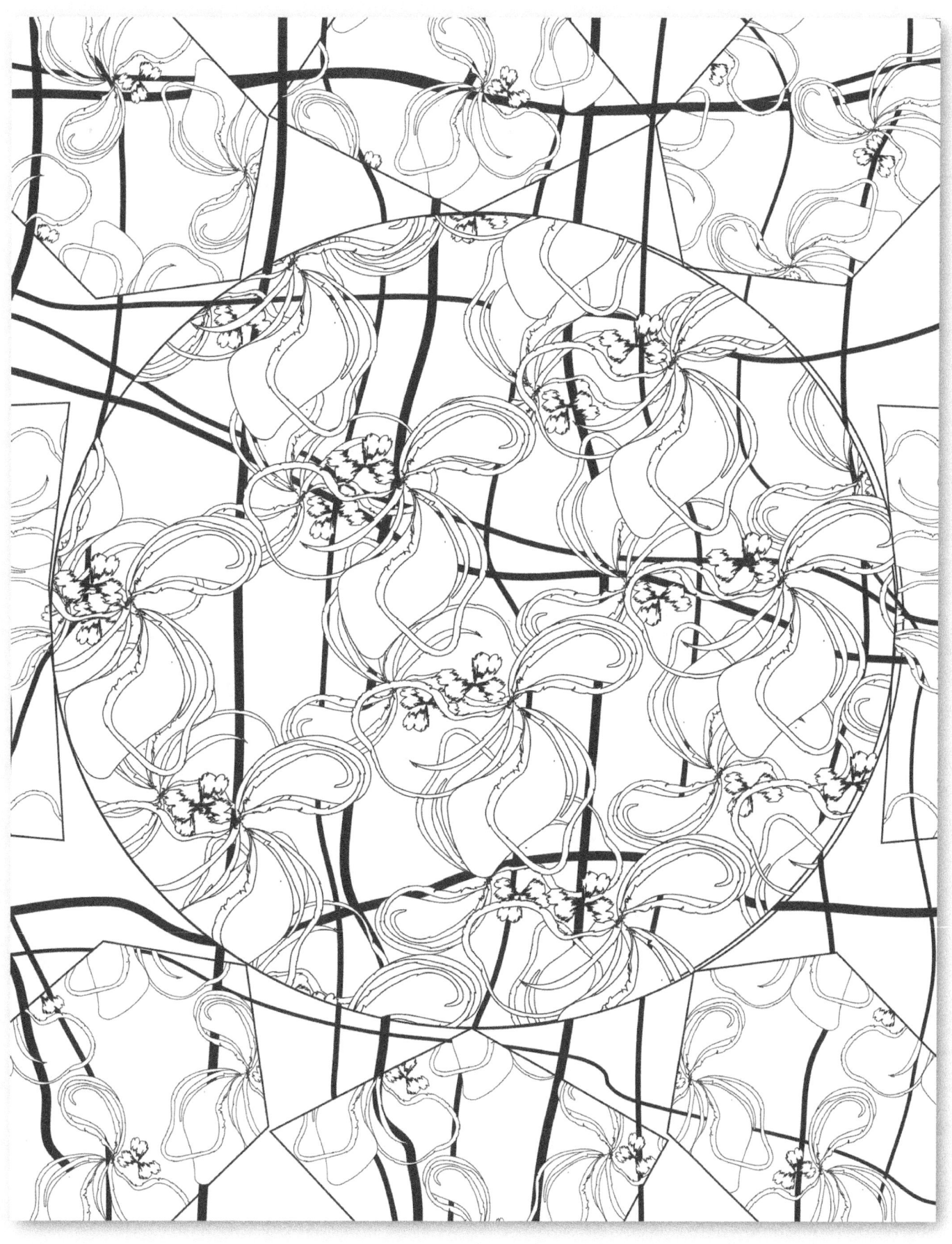

Barbara Jacobs

Your Notes and Drawings

Your Notes and Drawings

Color Journal Page

This page is a way for you to keep track of any favorite colors or color "blends."
Enjoy using this extra space for your own drawings, notes, or stories.
Feel free to use the spaces for actual colors, not just words.

<u>Love this color</u>   <u>Mixed with this color</u>   <u>Result is this color</u>

Used on this page_____

Used these materials_____

What I love about this color or combination of colors_____

Makes me feel_____

Today you are you! That is truer than true!
There is no one alive
who is you-er than you!

—Dr. Seuss

Express Your Moods, Create Your Stories

Explore, and Imagine

Part of making the most of your color expressions is in how you use color, and the goal here is to inspire you to explore. This process really takes us out of the busy-ness of our daily lives and helps bring our focus inward to a place where it seems we're not focusing at all, but are just getting into the colors, the feelings, and whatever comes up.

In spite of color theory and color psychology, in this experience there are No Rules at All! What can that mean for you? Just pick the color that speaks to you, that says to you "Here I am, now Pick Me Up and Color!" And, *that will be the right color for that time.* It's perfectly fine and in fact is a very natural, instinctive way to work. I like to call it "Play."

Another approach is to explore the feelings you want to create in each picture. Is it Bright and Sunny, or Stormy, or Shifting Moods; Courageous, or Careful, or a bit of both? And, which parts of the picture will express which feelings?

For the more analytical times, slow down before you start and think a bit about how your feelings correspond to the shapes of the image. Consider the colors you want to use to represent these feelings. We call these color selections your "color palette," which refers to the group or type of colors you'll select to use. You can even begin by selecting one group of three to five colors instead of one color at a time, and then add more as you want to emphasize or even change something completely.

When one is not instinctively called to select one color or another, it's sometimes hard to make the first choice so jump-starting the color selection with an intentional decision might help. OR: close your eyes and just pick one!

Use your colors as "seasonings" to add flavor!

Once you get into it, including just a little of an opposite feeling or mood will punctuate and complement the main group and make it even more meaningful. Think of using color as seasonings, as introducing flavors that enhance the whole.

A few "moods and emotions" you can communicate through color:

- Bright and Sunny
- Flavors – Sweet, Salty, Sour, Bitter, Pungent
- Temperature – Hot to Cold
- Weather – Stormy, Mild, Cloudy
- Light – Bright, Shadowed, Dark
- Shifting Moods

- Scary, Safe, Threatening
- Courageous
- Careful
- Happy, Joyful, Exuberant
- These are just a starting point – Add your own to the mix!

Interpret the image-stories or tell your own stories in line and color. Use the *Color Journal* page after each image. There is space to make doodles or pictures, write a few statements or a story, and record your favorite colors, color blends, and materials, as a reference for your next coloring projects.

> *Color can raise the dead!*
> —Iris Apfel (noted fashion maven)

—⚏—

I think the thing to do is enjoy the ride
while you're on it.

—Johnny Depp

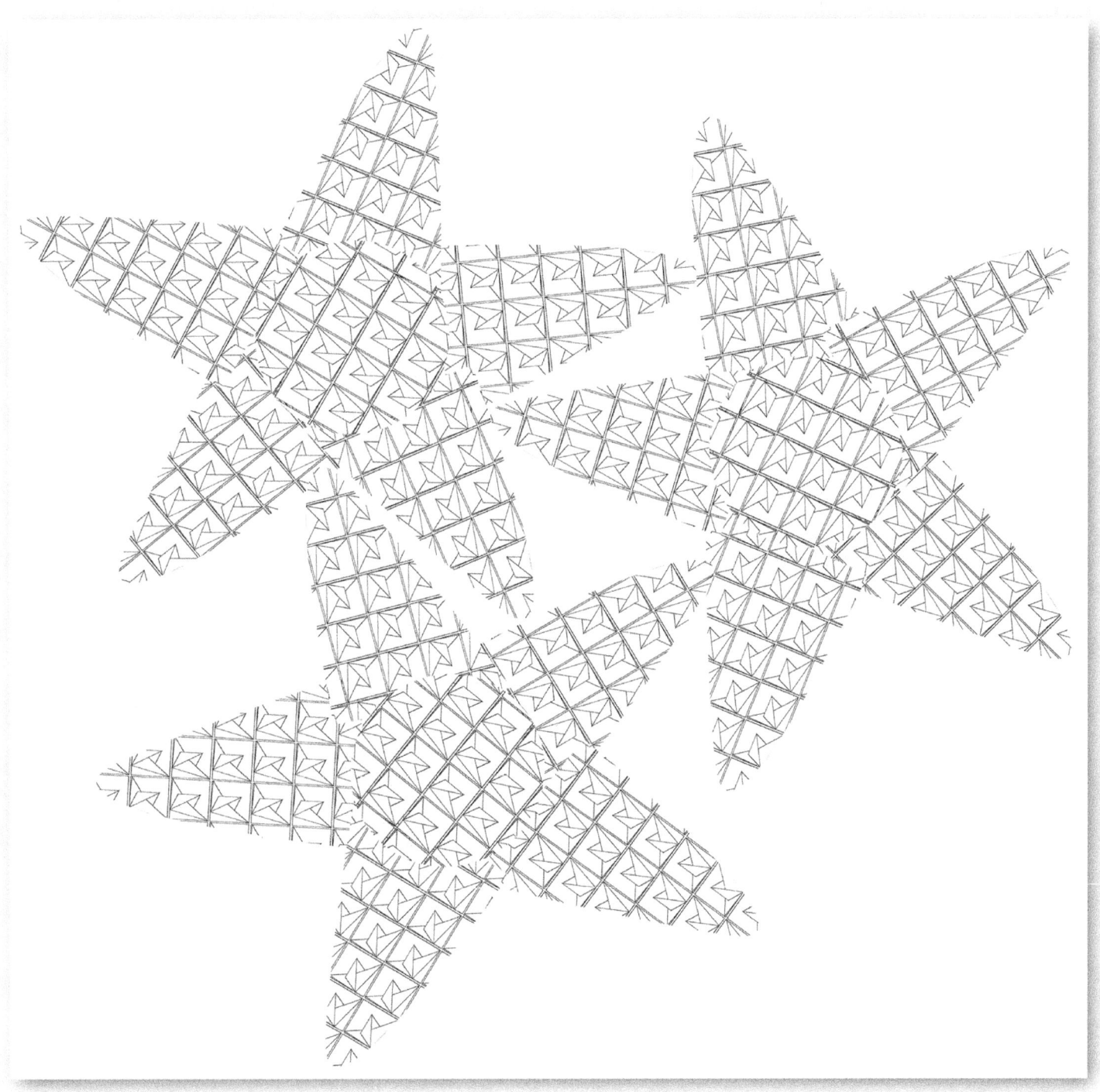

Barbara Jacobs

Your Notes and Drawings

Color Journal Page

This page is a way for you to keep track of any favorite colors or color "blends."
Enjoy using this extra space for your own drawings, notes, or stories.
Feel free to use the spaces for actual colors, not just words.

Love this color	Mixed with this color	Result is this color

Used on this page_____

Used these materials_____

What I love about this color or combination of colors_____

Makes me feel_____

Barbara Jacobs

The soul becomes dyed with
the color of its thoughts.

—Marcus Aurelius

Color Associations and the Meanings of Colors

What is "applied color psychology?"

It is important to choose the best colors for our personal and work environments. The colors that surround us, that we live among and within, do have an effect on our moods and feelings and even contribute to physiological conditions like our heart rate. You may have heard the term "color psychology." That expression refers to the ways our bodies and our mental and emotional states respond to various colors in our surroundings. This also refers to how colors can be applied in various ways for mental health therapy and in physical healing: the mind-body connection. It's not just about using your personal "favorite colors" or trend colors; there is quite a bit of detail involved in this in-depth, scientific approach to color design.

In the area of art work, color can be applied with a high level of intention when the artist uses specific colors to communicate a message. In combining color with other elements of the work like strokes, shapes, textures, materials, and size, the artist can communicate very effectively on many levels. This is not just about two or three-dimensional art, but also extends to all other artistic media including film, music, theater, and dance, where the artist's use of color is an integral contributor to the audience's experience.

In the case of a coloring book—this one, or any others—the colorist (that's You!) can also decide to work with color in a variety of ways. Mainly, it's either intuitive or instinctive; 'from the gut,' or with intention and a plan. A combination of approaches is often most effective and might be the most natural way for you. I've created the illustrations in ***Windows to Imagination*** for you to color in *Your Way*, whatever it might be.

I've also included a "Color Associations Quiz" that I created for students in various seminars I've taught over the years. It is about using color in spaces where we live or work. This version includes the answers (at the end of this book), but there is space for you to add your own color notes according to the descriptions given. This reference tool is about colors and their meanings, associations, and effects, and is one that my students have enjoyed applying in their own artistic and design practices.

Using the color wheel as a reference – not a rule

In the basic color wheel shown on the back cover, the Primary and Secondary colors are labeled. Other mixes are in between those, and you can interpret how to mix them by adding one primary to the other, in varying degrees. That is where you may want to experiment, and make notes about your favorite colors that you have mixed yourself by either layering colored pencils or combining watercolors. Watercolor paints may bleed though this paper.

Express your feelings with color!

Refer to your instincts, or to the 'Color Associations Quiz" page, if you want to plan your palette for coloring a particular image. Happy and cheerful? Sad, angry, dreamy, pensive…

A "monochromatic" palette consists of a range of colors that are close together. Examples are groups of the warmer yellows, orange/reds, and their variants; or "blues/violets," or a range of greens. This type of color palette will produce a more one-sided feeling or statement. If you do find yourself drawn to a certain set of similar colors, consider which to choose that is an opposite, to use in smaller amounts that will bring drama to your overall work and emphasize your original color selections.

Using color to express your ideas.
When you study each picture you'll see groups of lines and images that work together in ways that appeal to you. Use color to emphasize these shapes as a way of refining your expression. In the instances where there is the duplicate of an image that is upside-down, explore how to communicate an entirely different end result or set of ideas and feelings.

See the section on *Looking, Seeing, Imagining* – for suggestions on viewing these alternate, second versions of each of the image pages.

—〜—

Barbara Jacobs

I spilt spot remover on my dog and he disappeared.

—Jack Benny

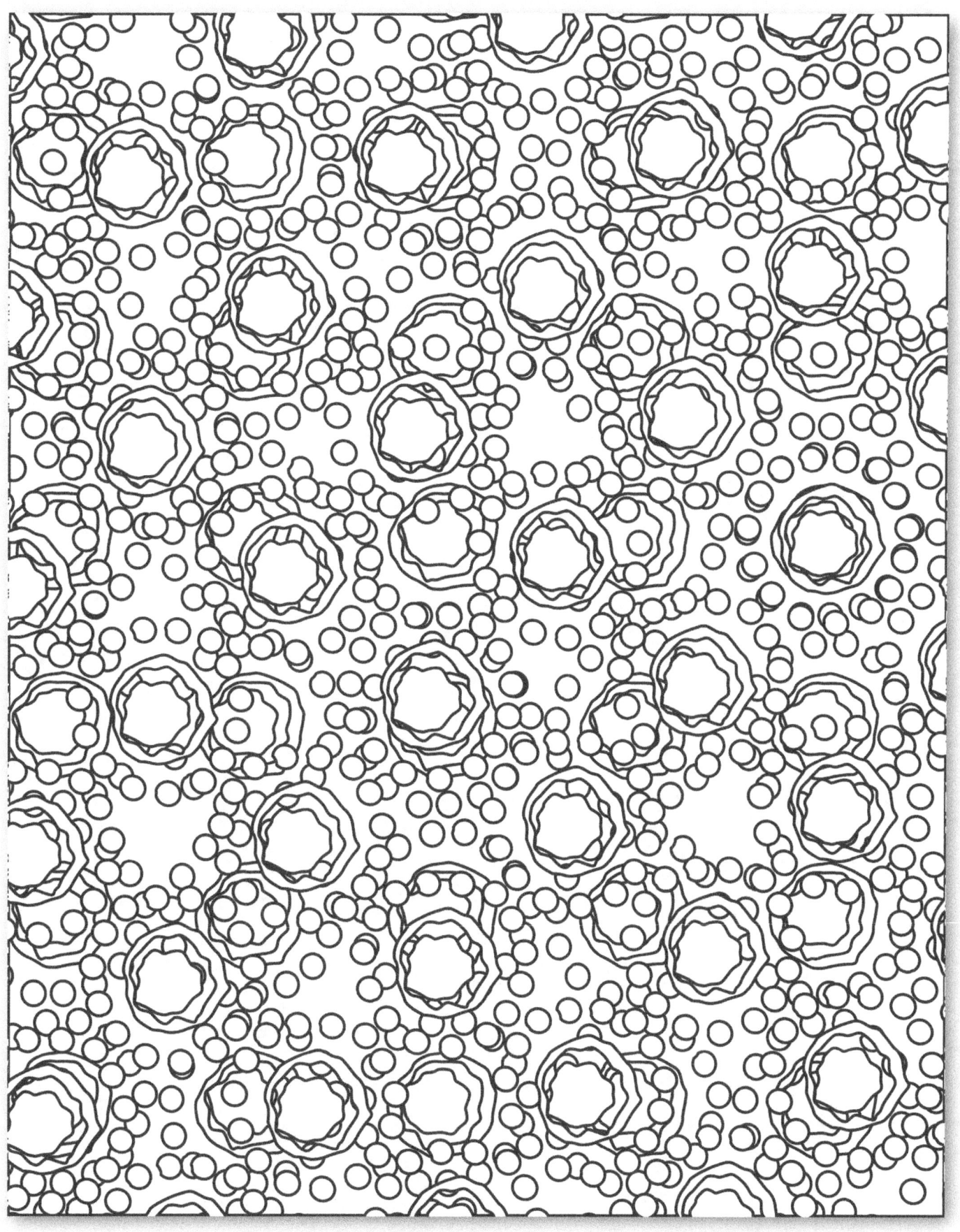

Barbara Jacobs

Your Notes and Drawings

Color Journal Page

This page is a way for you to keep track of any favorite colors or color "blends."
Enjoy using this extra space for your own drawings, notes, or stories.
Feel free to use the spaces for actual colors, not just words.

<u>Love this color</u>   <u>Mixed with this color</u>   <u>Result is this color</u>

Used on this page_____

Used these materials_____

What I love about this color or combination of colors_____

Makes me feel_____

*The hardest thing to see is
what is in front of your eyes.*

—Goethe

Part One
Fantastical Voyages

A series of fourteen drawings with the focus on hands and nature.
A color journal page follows each image.

Colour is a power which directly influences the soul. Colour is the keyboard, the eyes the hammer, the soul is the piano with many strings. The artist is the hand which places, touching one key or another to cause vibration in the soul. It is therefore evident that colour harmony must rest only on a corresponding vibration in the human soul.

—W.Kandinsky, *Concerning the Spriritual in Art*,
Wittenborn Schultz, New York, 1947

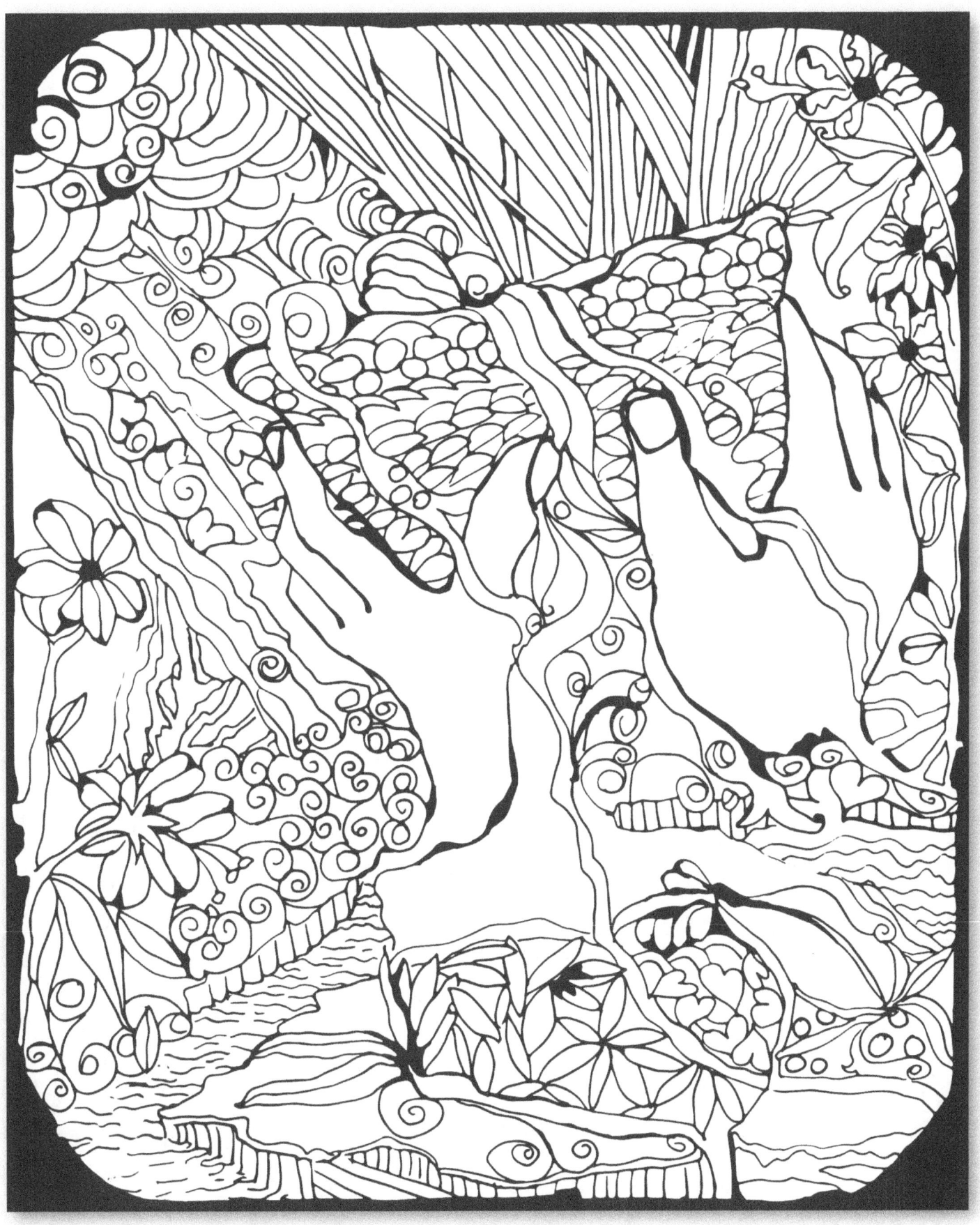

Barbara Jacobs

Your Notes and Drawings

Color Journal Page

This page is a way for you to keep track of any favorite colors or color "blends."
Enjoy using this extra space for your own drawings, notes, or stories.
Feel free to use the spaces for actual colors, not just words.

<u>Love this color</u>   <u>Mixed with this color</u>   <u>Result is this color</u>

Used on this page_____

Used these materials_____

What I love about this color or combination of colors_____

Makes me feel_____

Barbara Jacobs

All great artists draw from the same resource: the human heart,
which tells us that we are all more alike
than we are unalike.

—Maya Angelou

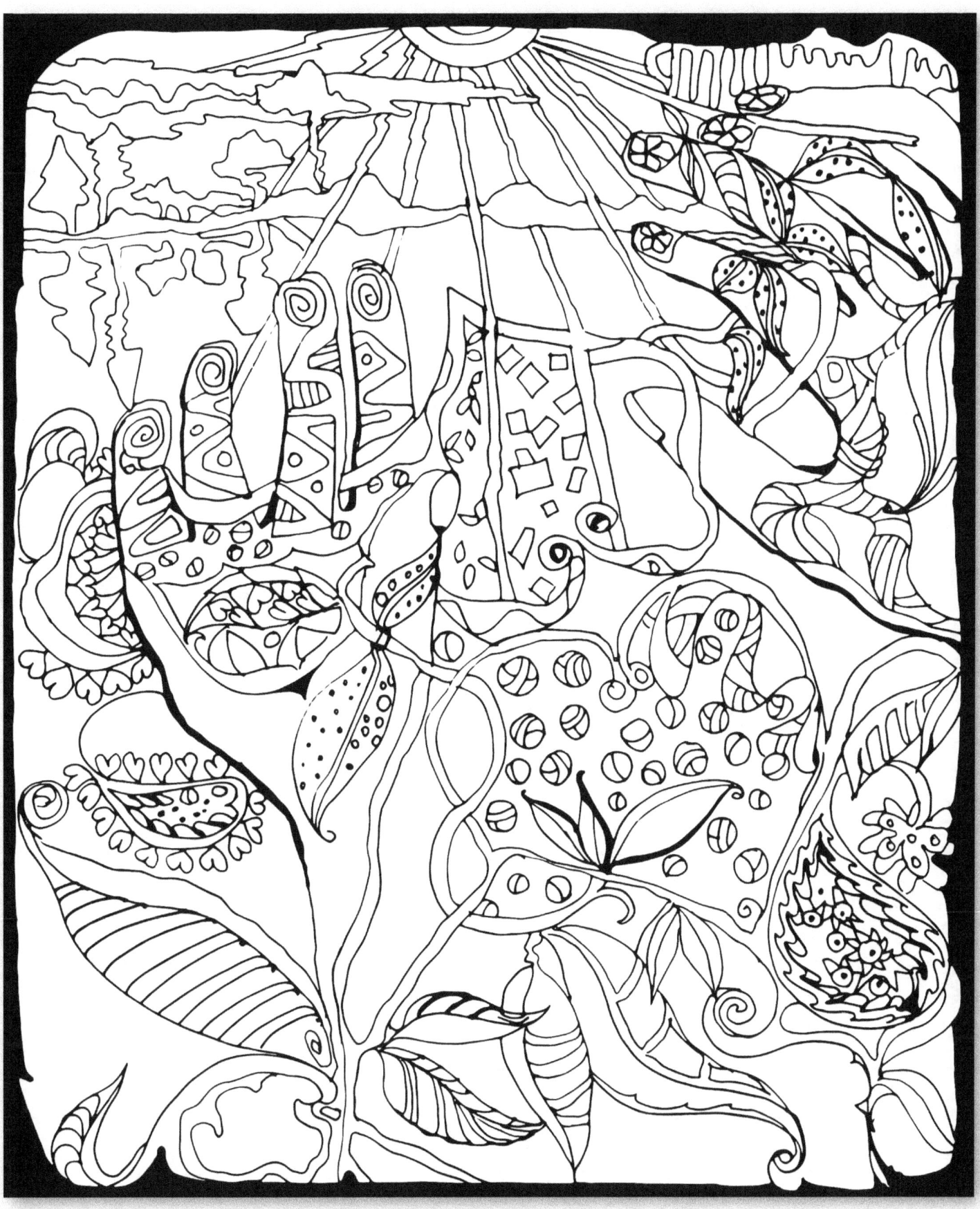

Barbara Jacobs

Your Notes and Drawings

Color Journal Page

This page is a way for you to keep track of any favorite colors or color "blends."
Enjoy using this extra space for your own drawings, notes, or stories.
Feel free to use the spaces for actual colors, not just words.

<u>Love this color</u>   <u>Mixed with this color</u>   <u>Result is this color</u>

Used on this page_____

Used these materials_____

What I love about this color or combination of colors_____

Makes me feel_____

Love comes in at the eye.

—W.B. Yeats

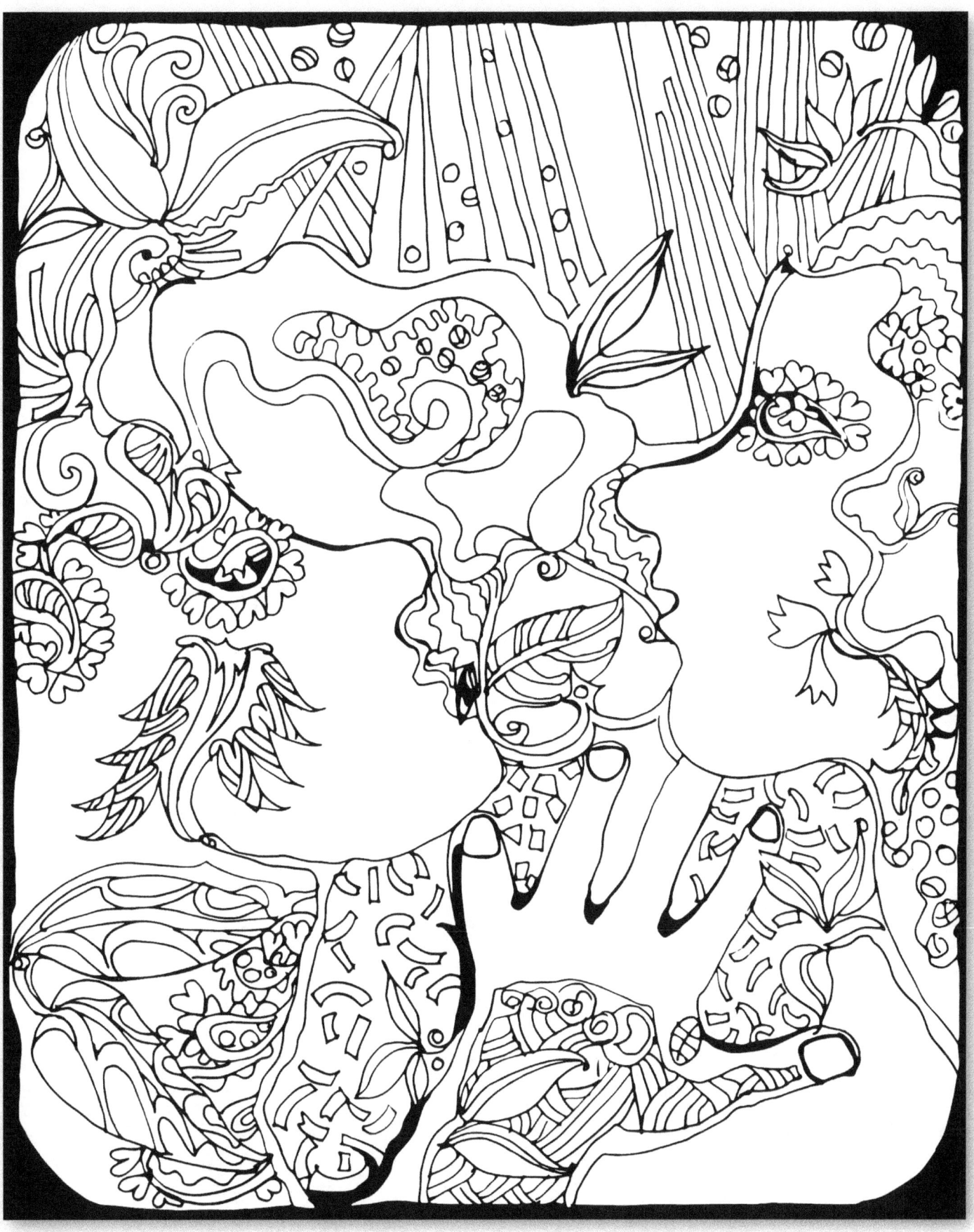

Barbara Jacobs

Your Notes and Drawings

Your Notes and Drawings

Color Journal Page

This page is a way for you to keep track of any favorite colors or color "blends."
Enjoy using this extra space for your own drawings, notes, or stories.
Feel free to use the spaces for actual colors, not just words.

<u>Love this color</u>   <u>Mixed with this color</u>   <u>Result is this color</u>

Used on this page_____

Used these materials_____

What I love about this color or combination of colors_____

Makes me feel_____

Barbara Jacobs

I feel through color.

—Henri Matisse

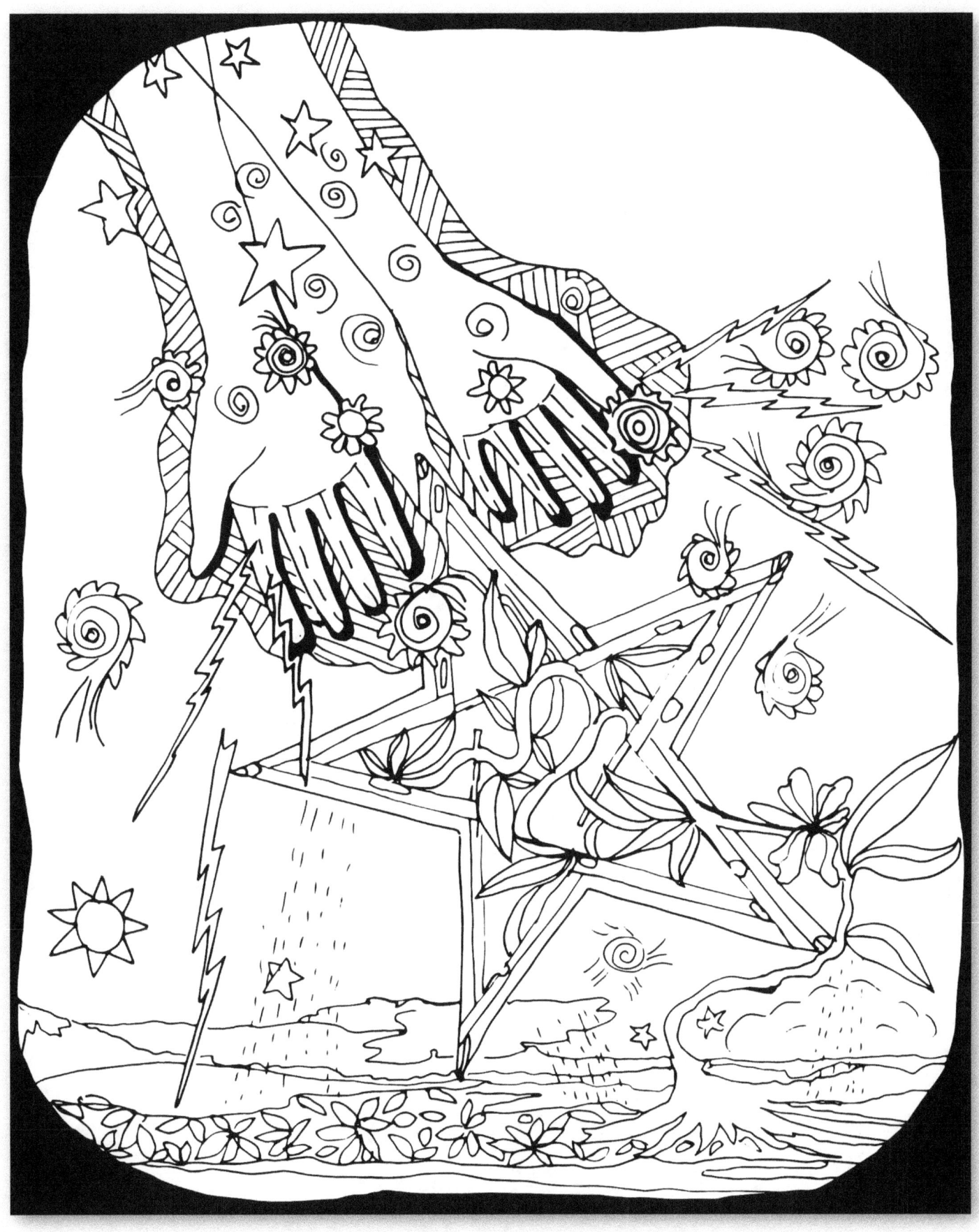

Barbara Jacobs

Your Notes and Drawings

Color Journal Page

This page is a way for you to keep track of any favorite colors or color "blends."
Enjoy using this extra space for your own drawings, notes, or stories.
Feel free to use the spaces for actual colors, not just words.

<u>Love this color</u>   <u>Mixed with this color</u>   <u>Result is this color</u>

Used on this page_____

Used these materials_____

What I love about this color or combination of colors_____

Makes me feel_____

Imagination rules the world.

—Napoleon Bonaparte

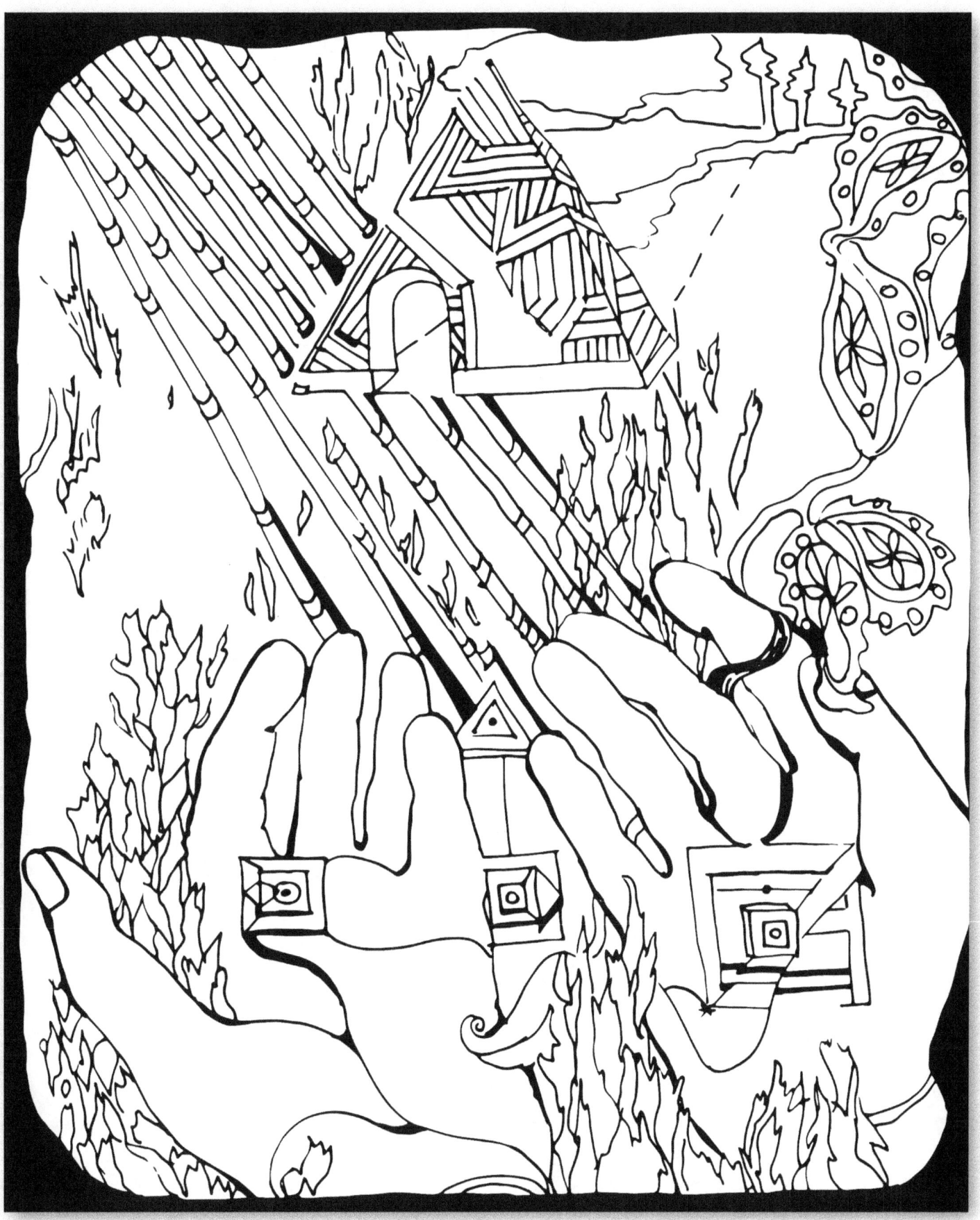

Barbara Jacobs

Your Notes and Drawings

Color Journal Page

This page is a way for you to keep track of any favorite colors or color "blends."
Enjoy using this extra space for your own drawings, notes, or stories.
Feel free to use the spaces for actual colors, not just words.

<u>Love this color</u>   <u>Mixed with this color</u>   <u>Result is this color</u>

Used on this page_____

Used these materials_____

What I love about this color or combination of colors_____

Makes me feel_____

Barbara Jacobs

Reality is wrong.
Dreams are for real.

—Tupac Shakur

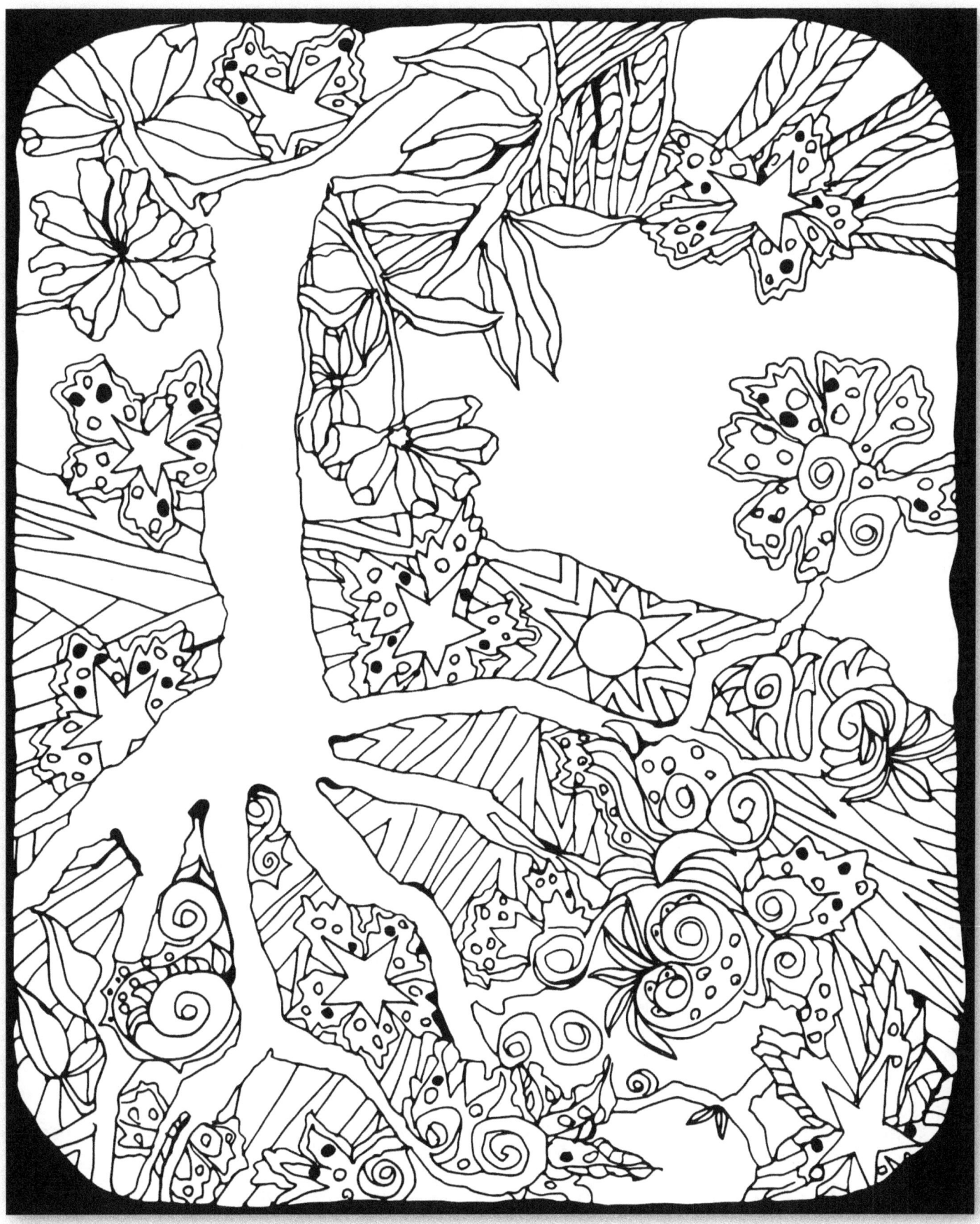

Barbara Jacobs

Your Notes and Drawings

Color Journal Page

This page is a way for you to keep track of any favorite colors or color "blends."
Enjoy using this extra space for your own drawings, notes, or stories.
Feel free to use the spaces for actual colors, not just words.

<u>Love this color</u>   <u>Mixed with this color</u>   <u>Result is this color</u>

Used on this page_____

Used these materials_____

What I love about this color or combination of colors_____

Makes me feel_____

*Vision is the art of
seeing things invisible.*

—Johnathan Swift

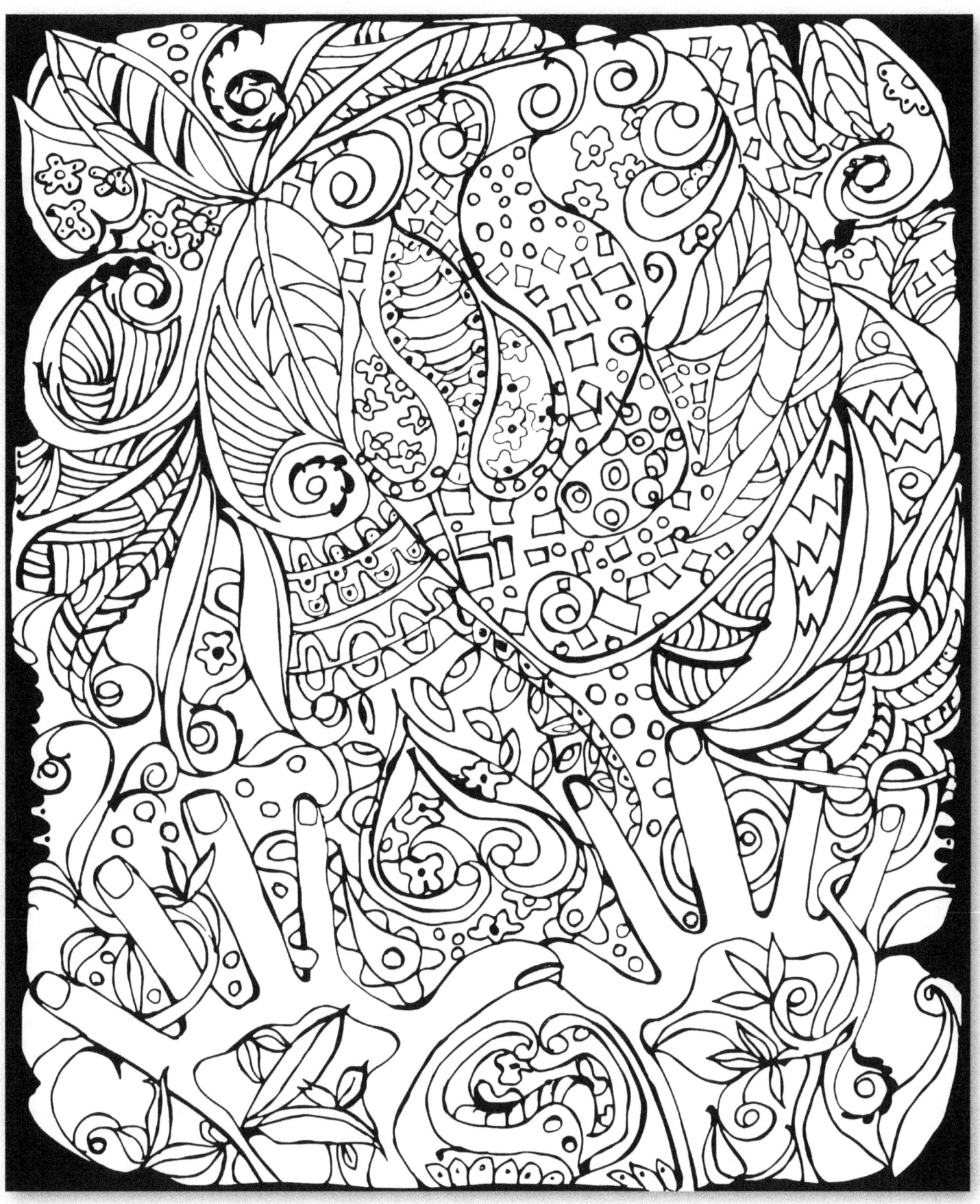

Barbara Jacobs

Your Notes and Drawings

Color Journal Page

This page is a way for you to keep track of any favorite colors or color "blends."
Enjoy using this extra space for your own drawings, notes, or stories.
Feel free to use the spaces for actual colors, not just words.

<u>Love this color</u>   <u>Mixed with this color</u>   <u>Result is this color</u>

Used on this page_____

Used these materials_____

What I love about this color or combination of colors_____

Makes me feel_____

I shut my eyes in order to see.

—Paul Gauguin

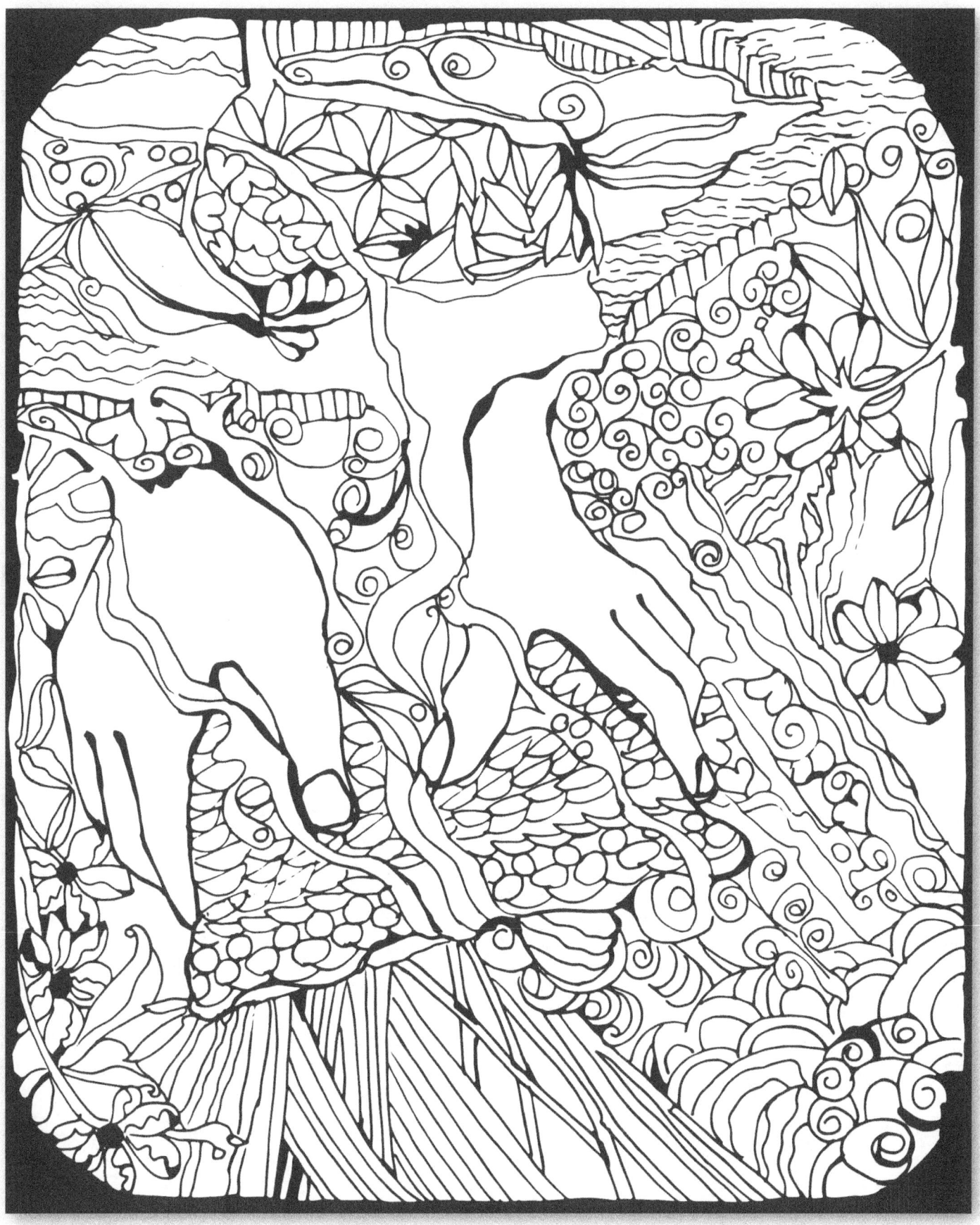

Barbara Jacobs

Your Notes and Drawings

Your Notes and Drawings

Color Journal Page

This page is a way for you to keep track of any favorite colors or color "blends."
Enjoy using this extra space for your own drawings, notes, or stories.
Feel free to use the spaces for actual colors, not just words.

<u>Love this color</u>   <u>Mixed with this color</u>   <u>Result is this color</u>

Used on this page_____

Used these materials_____

What I love about this color or combination of colors_____

Makes me feel_____

Form comes from wonder.

—Louis Kahn

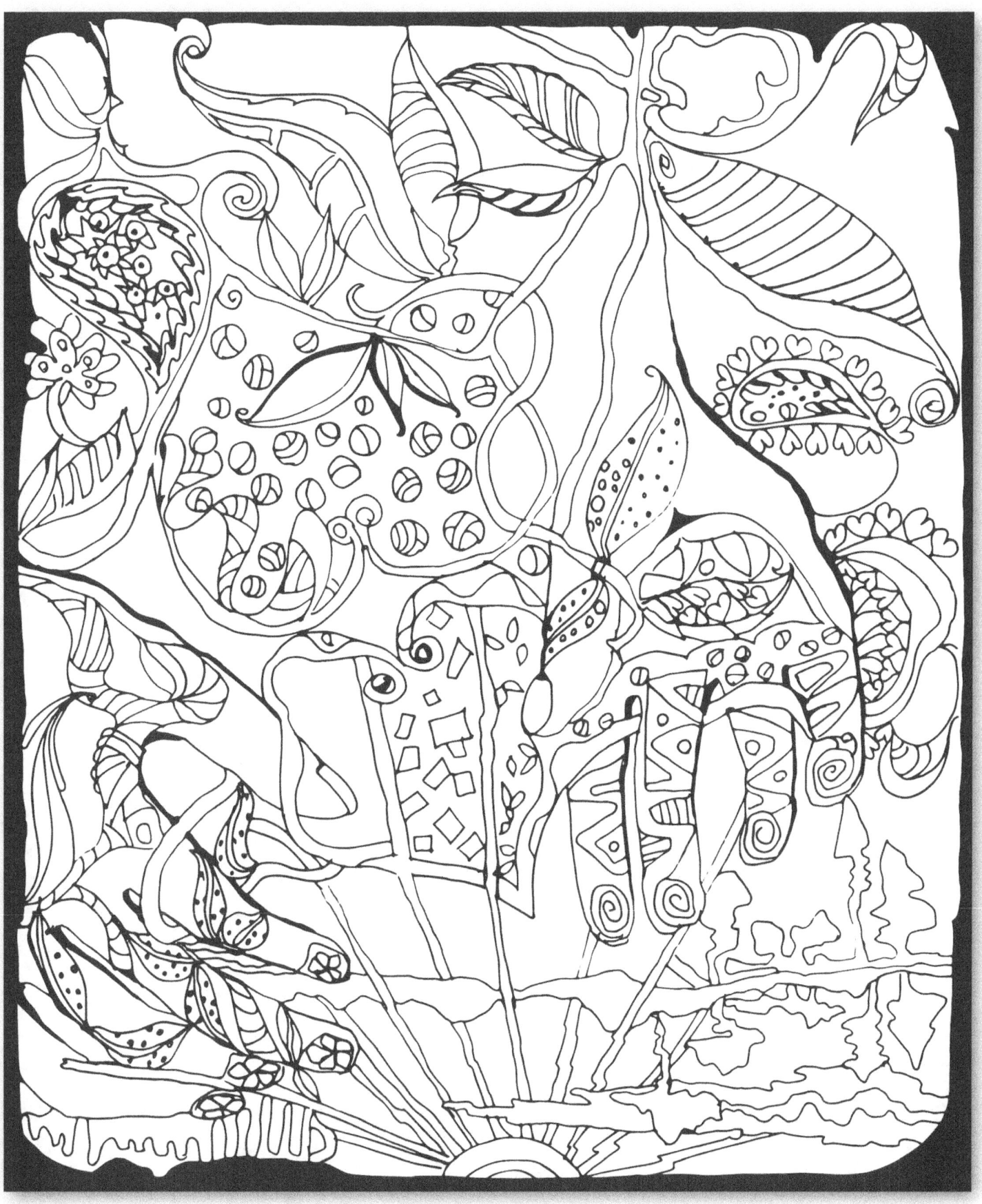

Barbara Jacobs

Your Notes and Drawings

Color Journal Page

This page is a way for you to keep track of any favorite colors or color "blends."
Enjoy using this extra space for your own drawings, notes, or stories.
Feel free to use the spaces for actual colors, not just words.

<u>Love this color</u>   <u>Mixed with this color</u>   <u>Result is this color</u>

Used on this page_____

Used these materials_____

What I love about this color or combination of colors_____

Makes me feel_____

Kindness is the language which the deaf can hear and the blind can see.

—Mark Twain

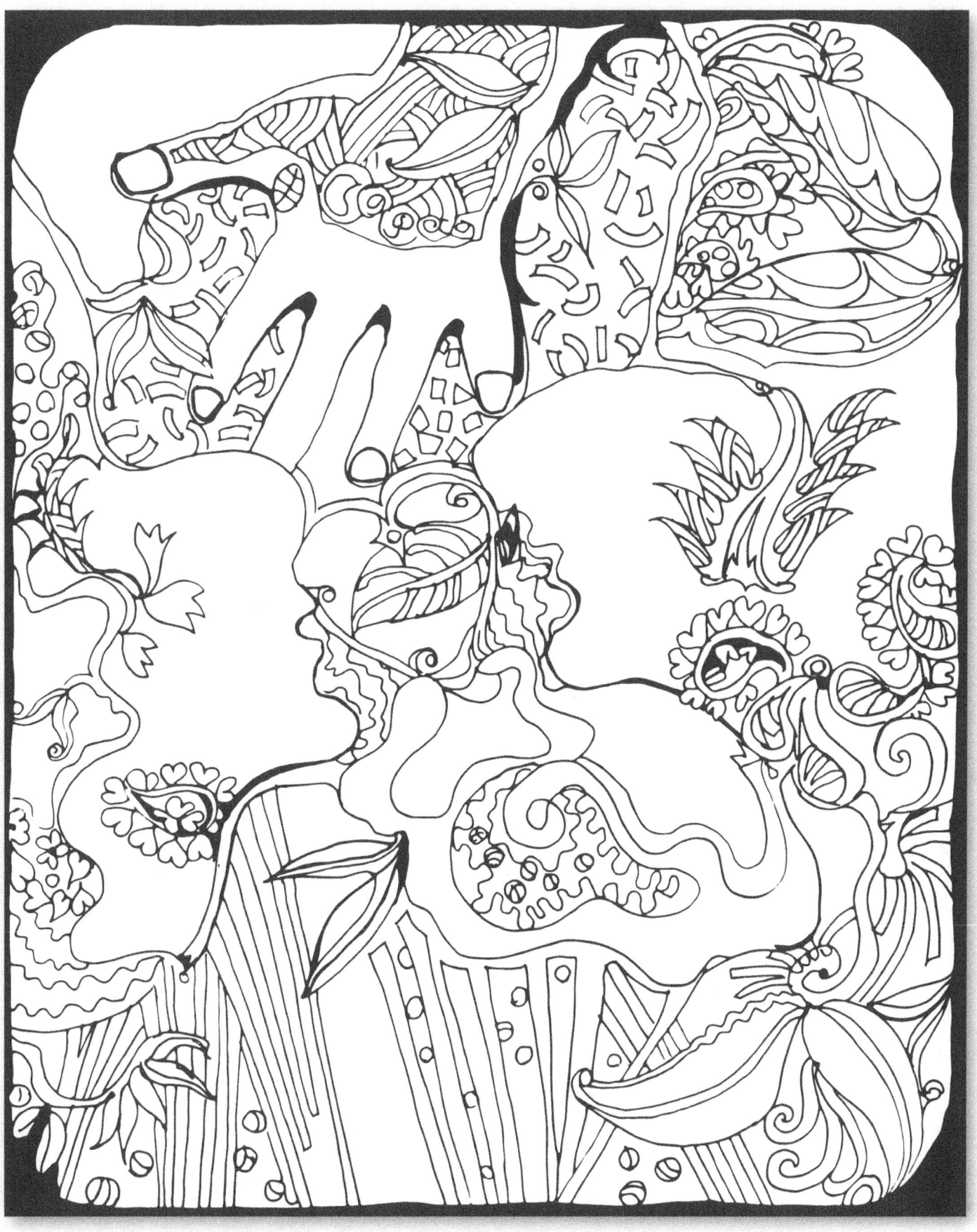

Barbara Jacobs

Your Notes and Drawings

Your Notes and Drawings

Color Journal Page

This page is a way for you to keep track of any favorite colors or color "blends."
Enjoy using this extra space for your own drawings, notes, or stories.
Feel free to use the spaces for actual colors, not just words.

<u>Love this color</u>   <u>Mixed with this color</u>   <u>Result is this color</u>

Used on this page_____

Used these materials_____

What I love about this color or combination of colors_____

Makes me feel_____

It is in your moments of decision that your destiny is shaped.

—Tony Robbins

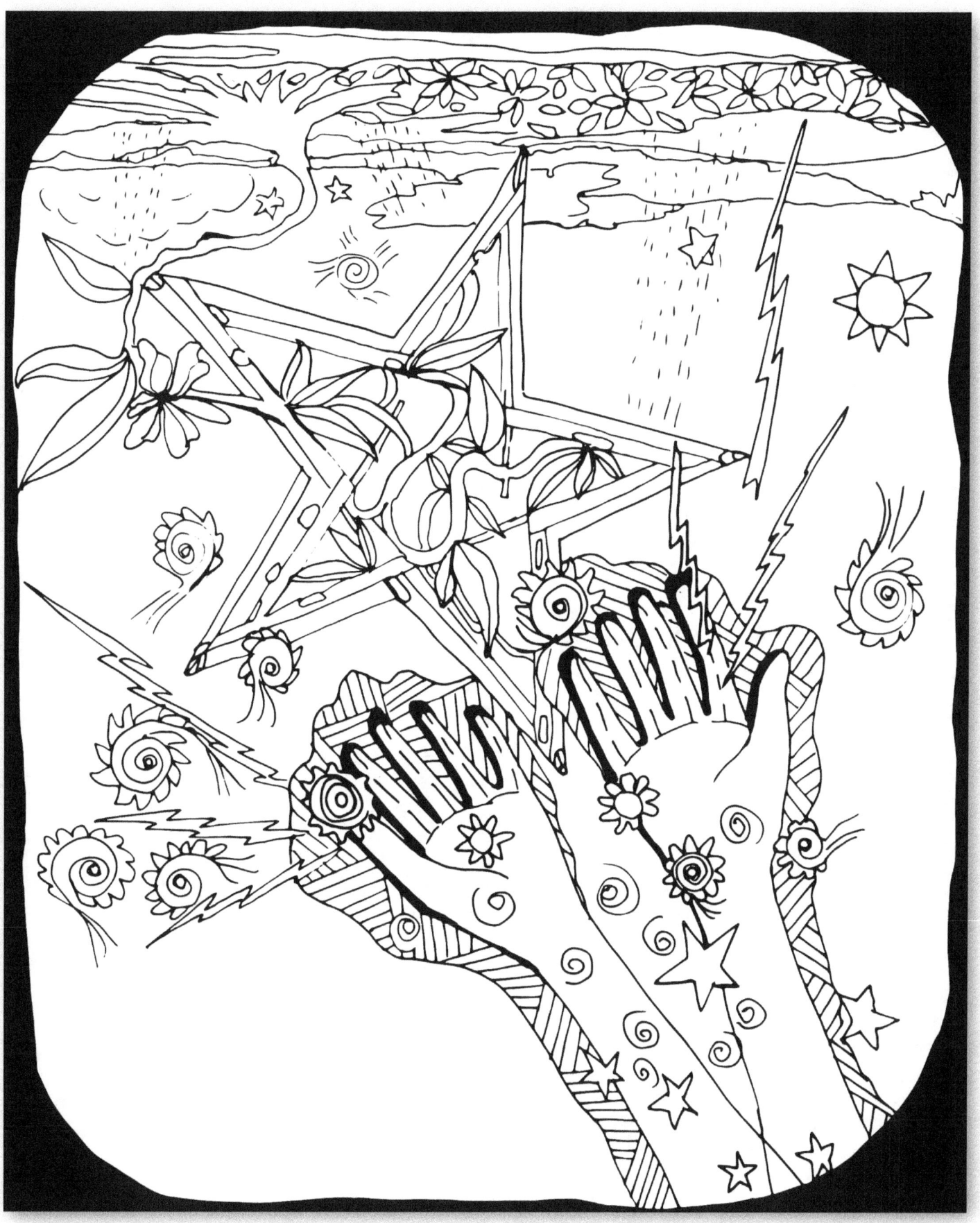

Barbara Jacobs

Your Notes and Drawings

Color Journal Page

This page is a way for you to keep track of any favorite colors or color "blends."
Enjoy using this extra space for your own drawings, notes, or stories.
Feel free to use the spaces for actual colors, not just words.

<u>Love this color</u>   <u>Mixed with this color</u>   <u>Result is this color</u>

Used on this page_____

Used these materials_____

What I love about this color or combination of colors_____

Makes me feel_____

I found I could say things with color and shapes that I couldn't say any other way – things I had no words for.

—Georgia O'Keeffe

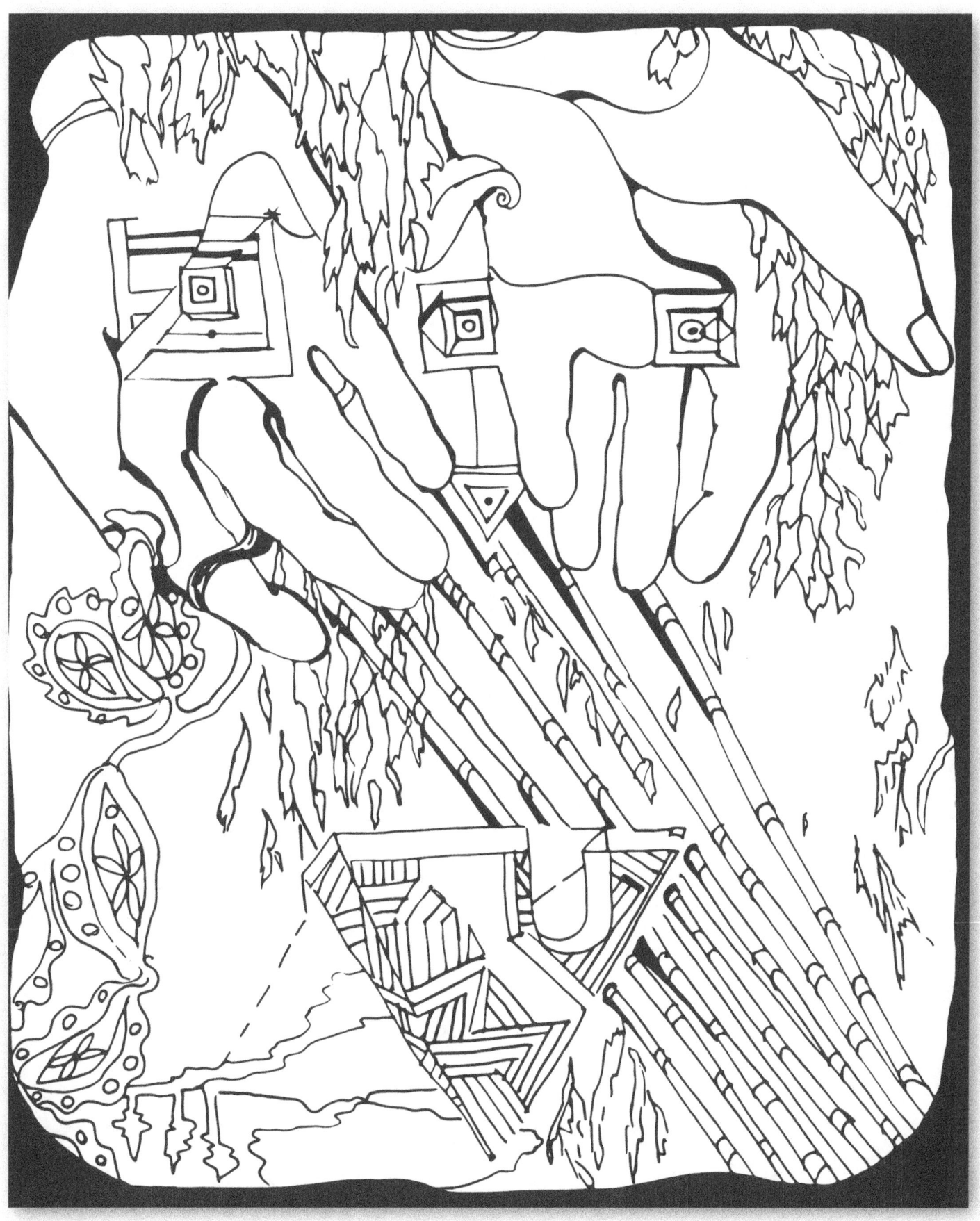

Barbara Jacobs

Your Notes and Drawings

Color Journal Page

This page is a way for you to keep track of any favorite colors or color "blends."
Enjoy using this extra space for your own drawings, notes, or stories.
Feel free to use the spaces for actual colors, not just words.

<u>Love this color</u>   <u>Mixed with this color</u>   <u>Result is this color</u>

Used on this page_____

Used these materials_____

What I love about this color or combination of colors_____

Makes me feel_____

*The artist's vocation is to send
light into the human heart.*

—George Sand

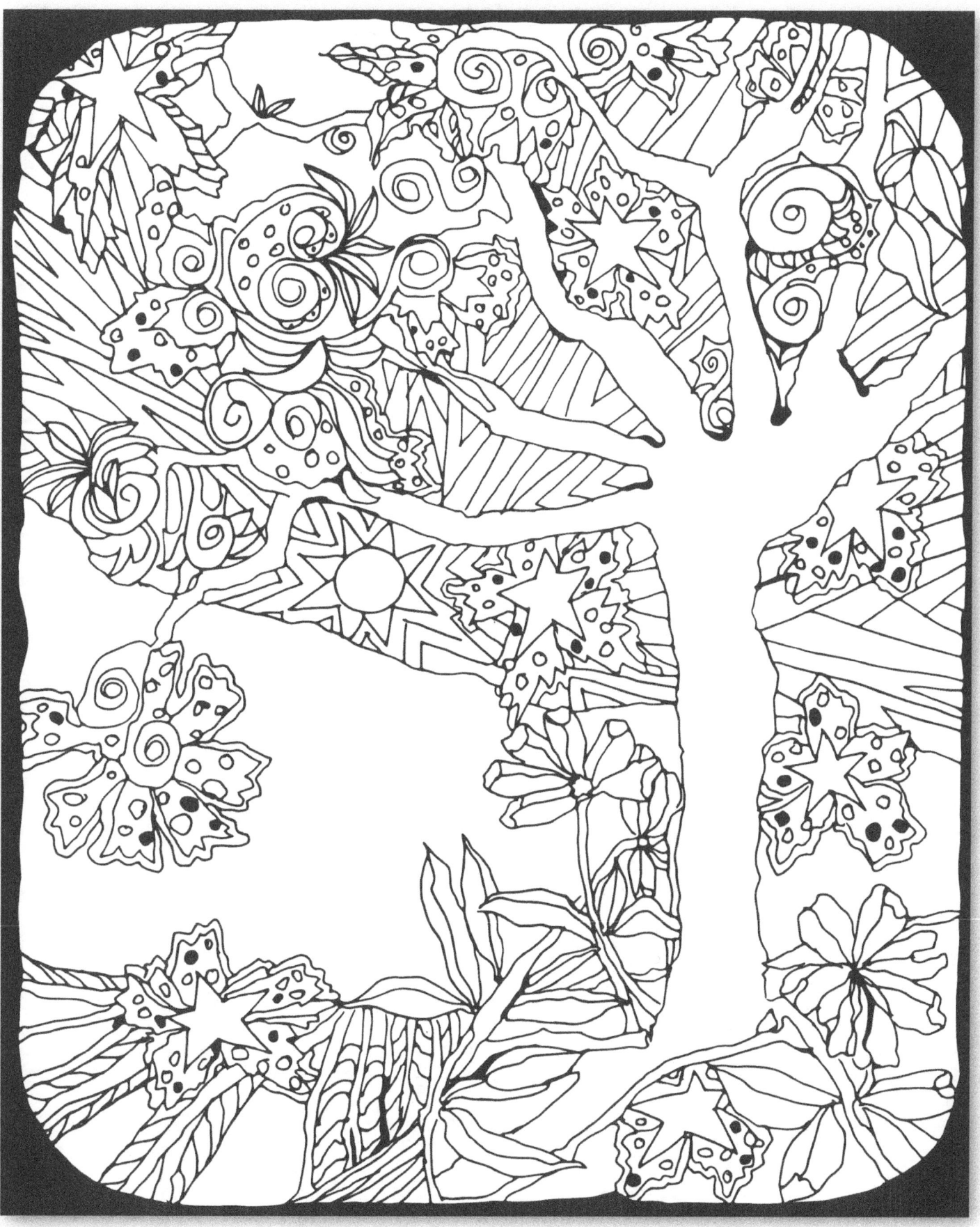

Barbara Jacobs

Your Notes and Drawings

Color Journal Page

This page is a way for you to keep track of any favorite colors or color "blends."
Enjoy using this extra space for your own drawings, notes, or stories.
Feel free to use the spaces for actual colors, not just words.

<u>Love this color</u>   <u>Mixed with this color</u>   <u>Result is this color</u>

Used on this page_____

Used these materials_____

What I love about this color or combination of colors_____

Makes me feel_____

Barbara Jacobs

What is art but a way of seeing?

—Saul Bellow

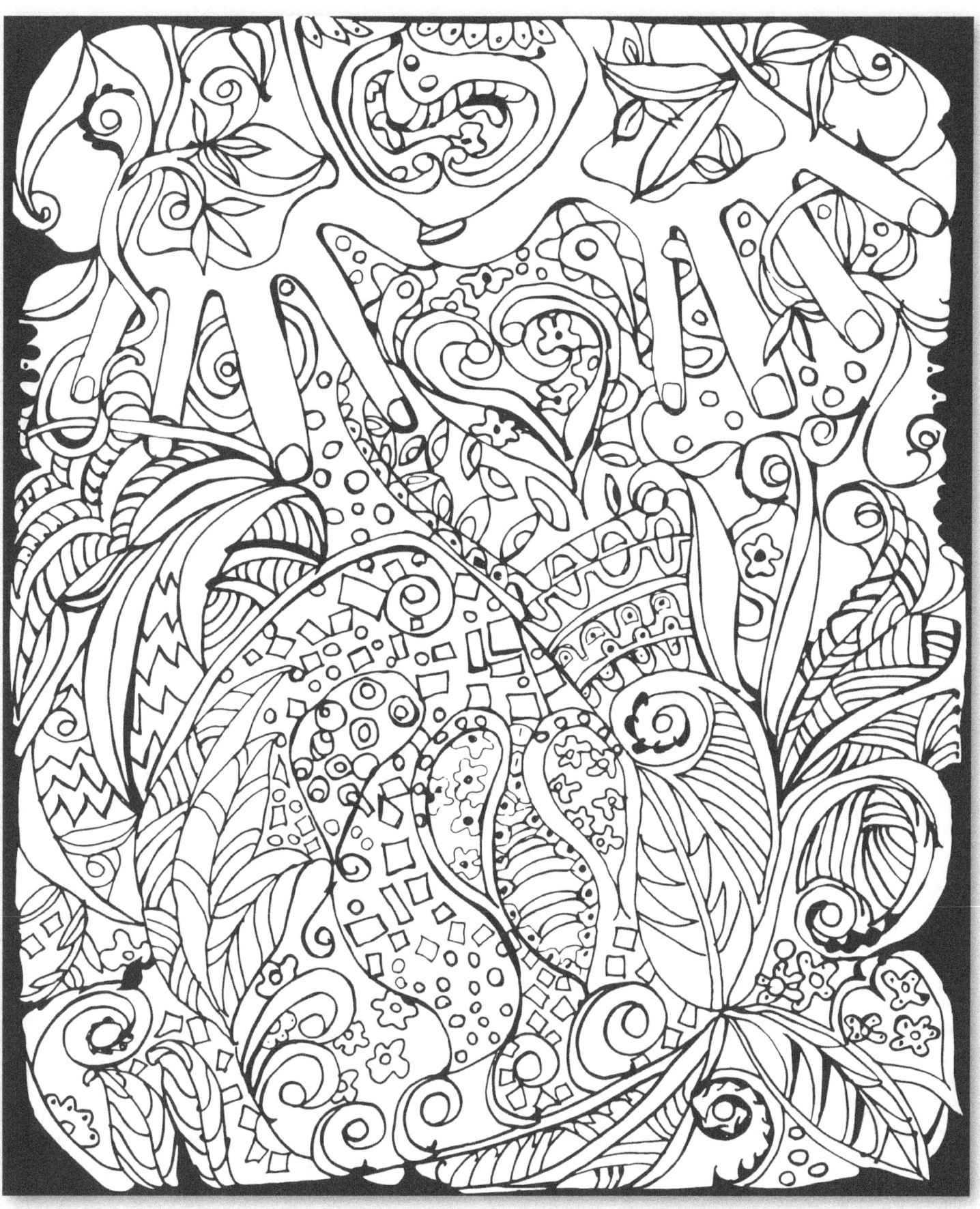

Barbara Jacobs

Your Notes and Drawings

Color Journal Page

This page is a way for you to keep track of any favorite colors or color "blends."
Enjoy using this extra space for your own drawings, notes, or stories.
Feel free to use the spaces for actual colors, not just words.

<u>**Love this color**</u>   <u>**Mixed with this color**</u>   <u>**Result is this color**</u>

Used on this page_____

Used these materials_____

What I love about this color or combination of colors_____

Makes me feel_____

A few thoughts on the concept of
'less is more...'

Less is only more when more is no good.

— Frank Lloyd Wright

Less is a bore.

—Robert Venturi

Less is a snore.

—Gianni Versaci

For me more is more

—Gianfranco Ferre

More matter with less art.

—William Shakespeare

Minus=Plus.

—Josef Albers

Part Two
Patterns

A varied series of twenty-one additional abstract pattern designs.
Some are digital, some are hand drawn.
A Note About Lines – Make Your Own Design!

Be Creative – go "outside the box."
Where you see unconnected or open-ended lines or shapes in any of the
patterns, you're invited to add your own connections.

Barbara Jacobs

I want to know one thing:
What is colour?

—Pablo Picasso

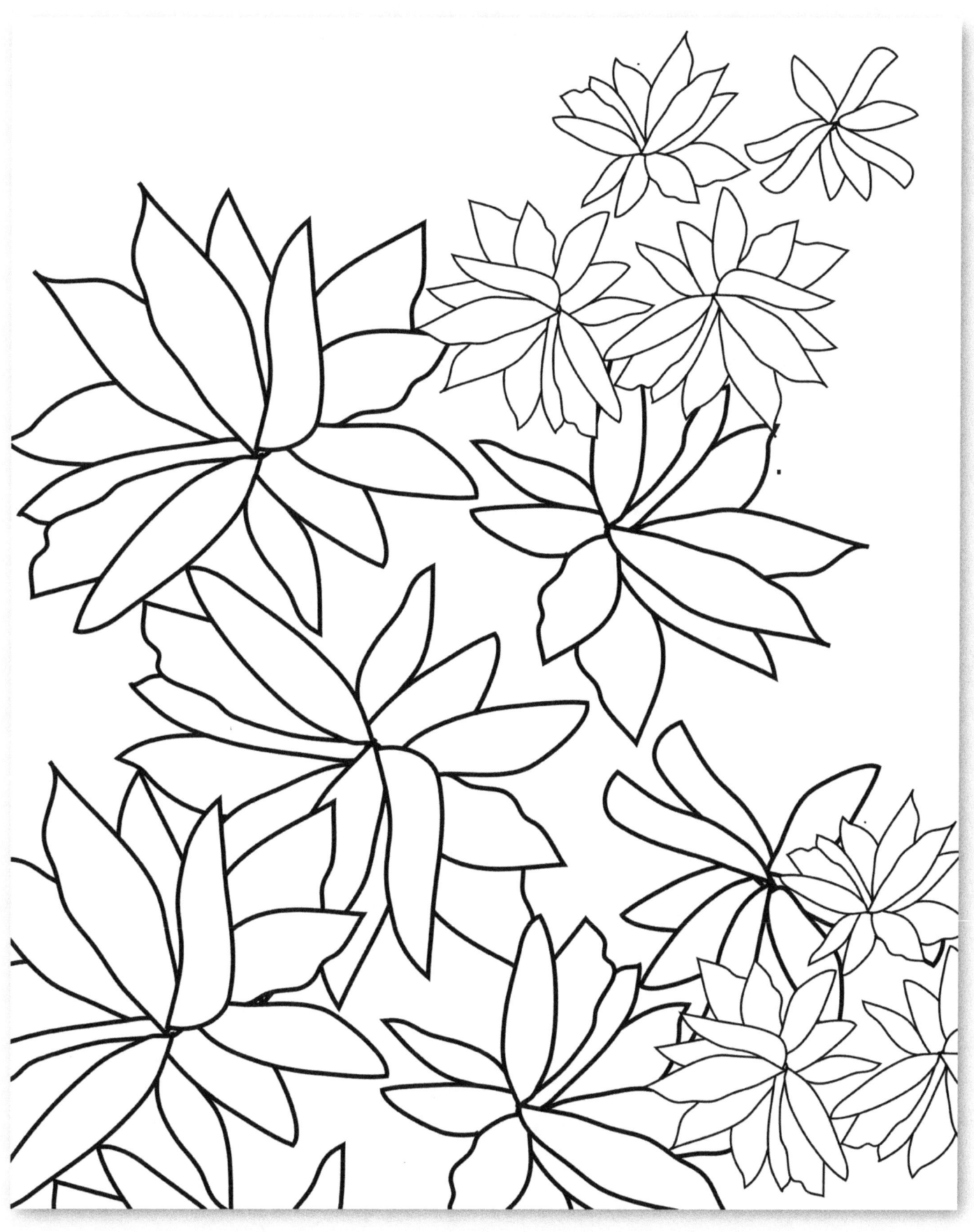

Barbara Jacobs

Your Notes and Drawings

Color Journal Page

This page is a way for you to keep track of any favorite colors or color "blends."
Enjoy using this extra space for your own drawings, notes, or stories.
Feel free to use the spaces for actual colors, not just words.

<u>Love this color</u>   <u>Mixed with this color</u>   <u>Result is this color</u>

Used on this page_____

Used these materials_____

What I love about this color or combination of colors_____

Makes me feel_____

Opportunities are like sunrises.
If you wait too long, you miss them.

—William Arthur Ward

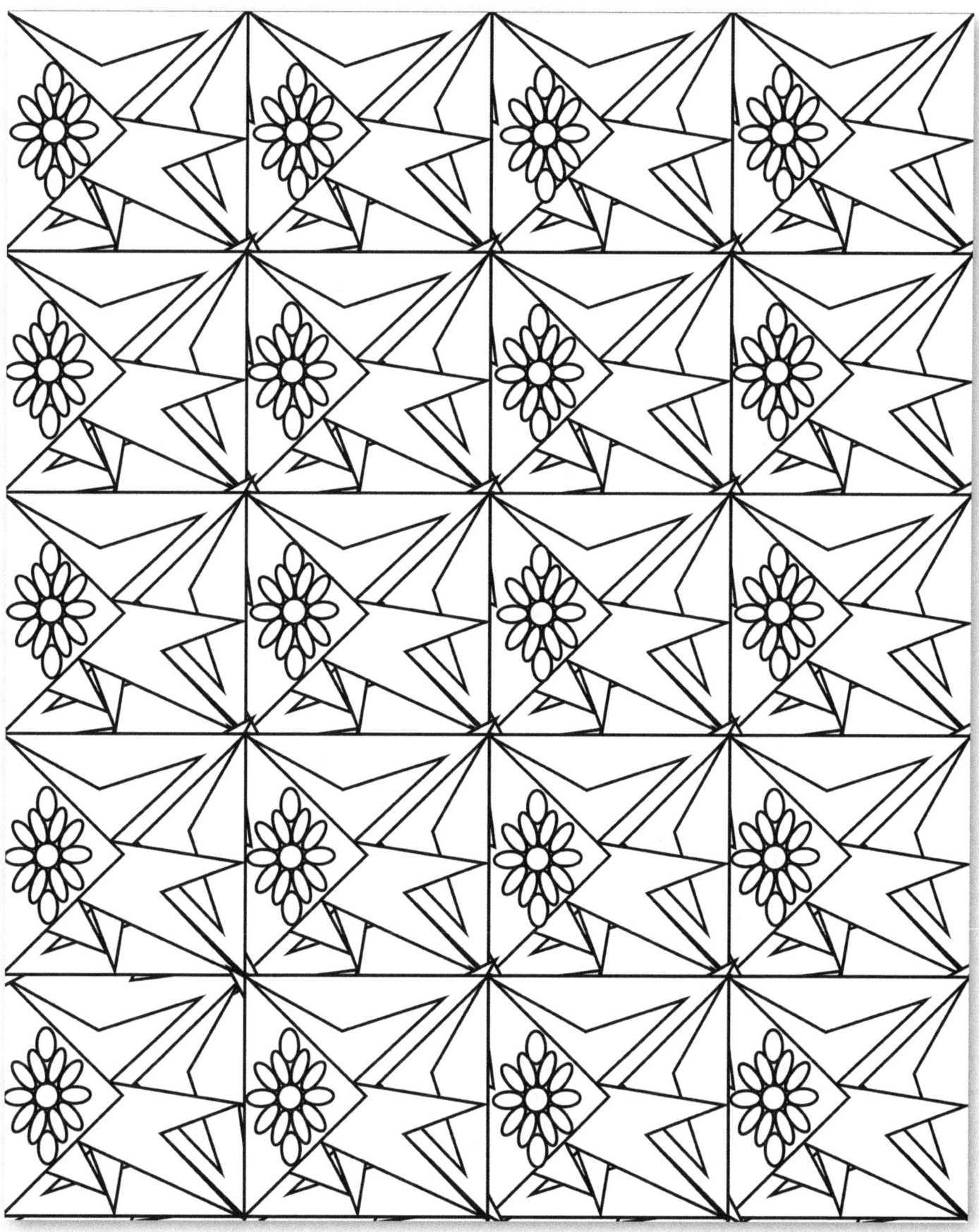

Barbara Jacobs

Your Notes and Drawings

Color Journal Page

This page is a way for you to keep track of any favorite colors or color "blends."
Enjoy using this extra space for your own drawings, notes, or stories.
Feel free to use the spaces for actual colors, not just words.

<u>Love this color</u>   <u>Mixed with this color</u>   <u>Result is this color</u>

Used on this page_____

Used these materials_____

What I love about this color or combination of colors_____

Makes me feel_____

Barbara Jacobs

First thing every morning before
you arise say out loud,
'I believe,' three times.

—Ovid

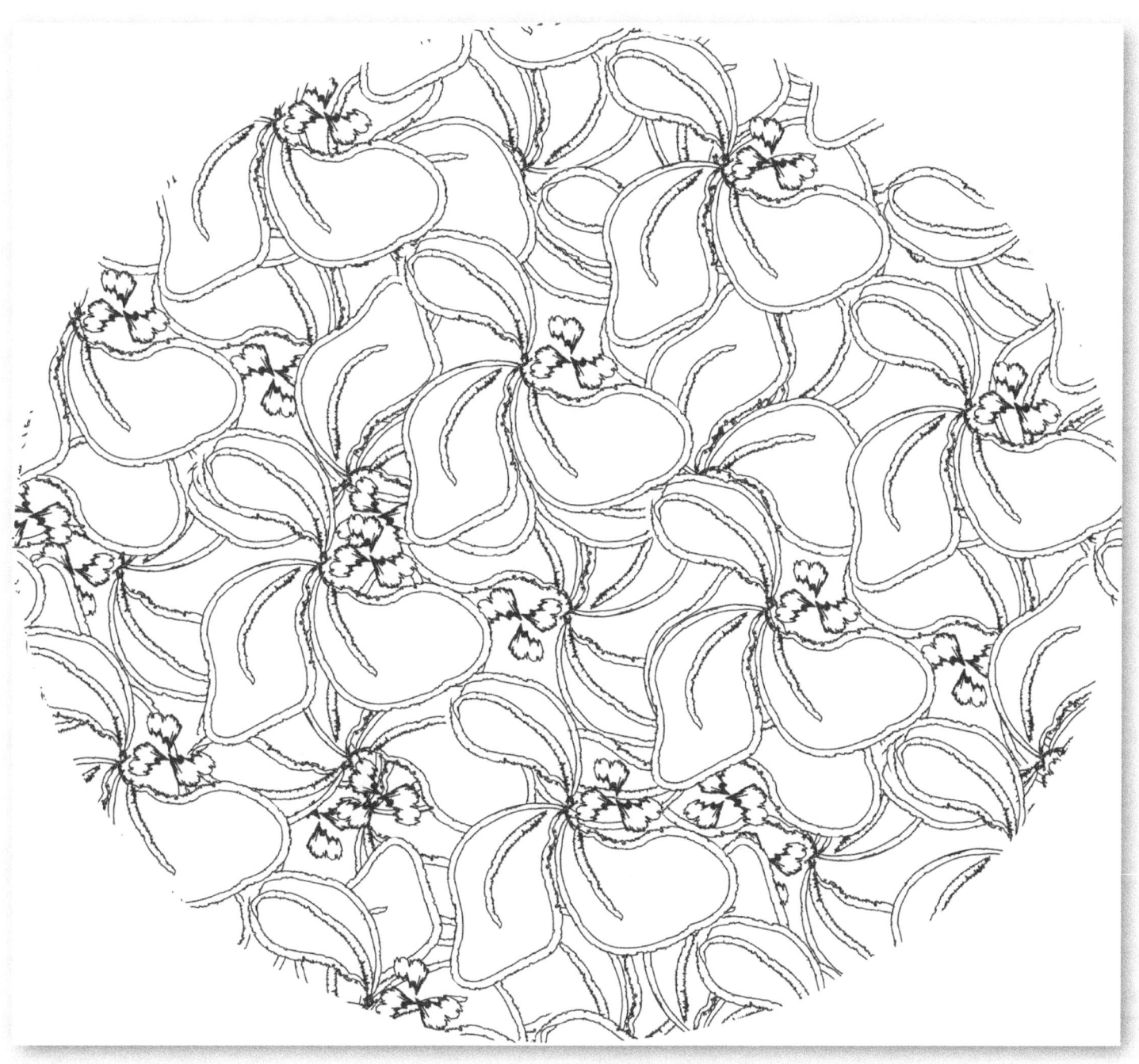

Barbara Jacobs

Your Notes and Drawings

Color Journal Page

This page is a way for you to keep track of any favorite colors or color "blends."
Enjoy using this extra space for your own drawings, notes, or stories.
Feel free to use the spaces for actual colors, not just words.

<u>Love this color</u>   <u>Mixed with this color</u>   <u>Result is this color</u>

Used on this page_____

Used these materials_____

What I love about this color or combination of colors_____

Makes me feel_____

When you're curious, you find lots of interesting things to do.

—Walt Disney

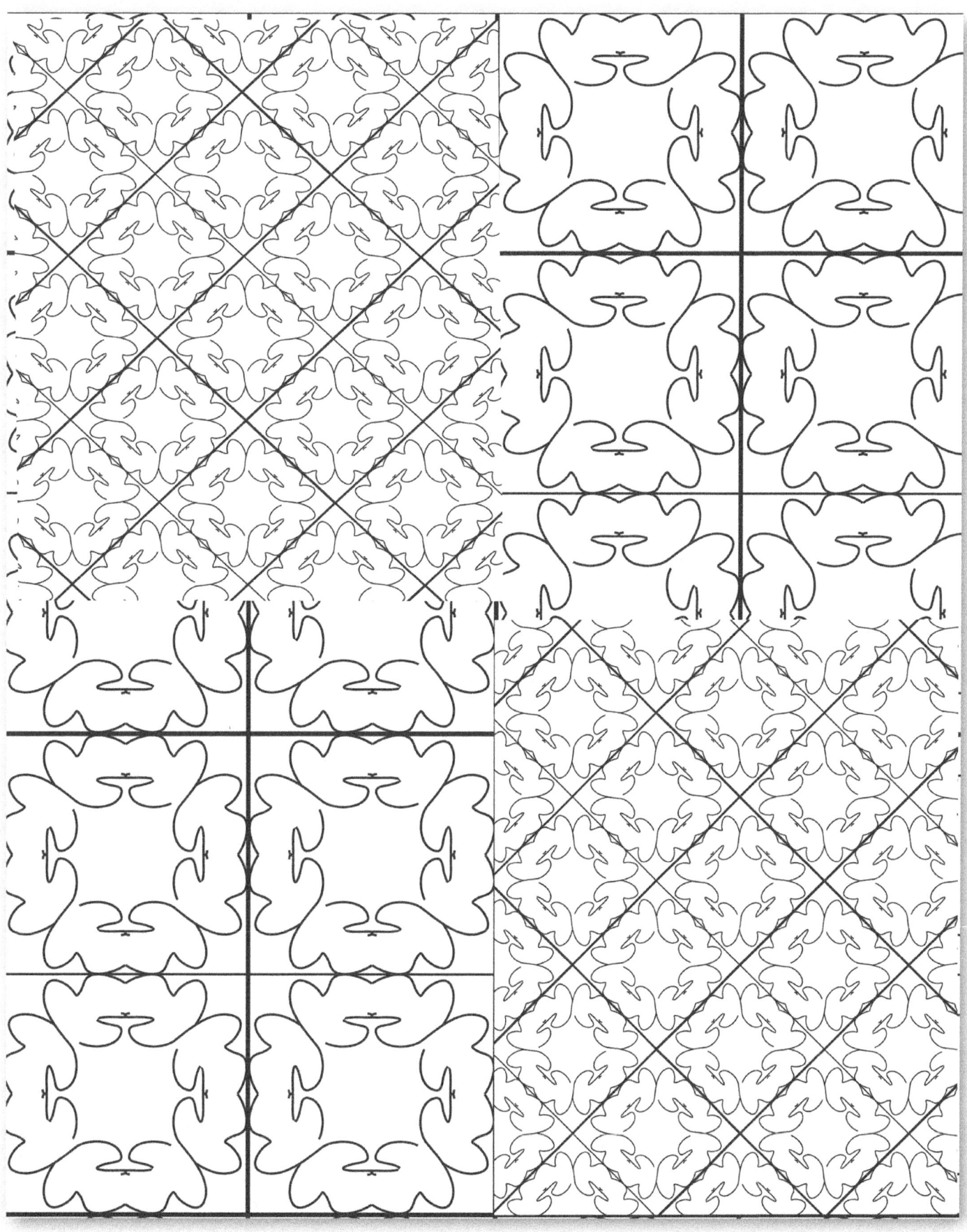

Barbara Jacobs

Your Notes and Drawings

Color Journal Page

This page is a way for you to keep track of any favorite colors or color "blends."
Enjoy using this extra space for your own drawings, notes, or stories.
Feel free to use the spaces for actual colors, not just words.

<u>Love this color</u>   <u>Mixed with this color</u>   <u>Result is this color</u>

Used on this page_____

Used these materials_____

What I love about this color or combination of colors_____

Makes me feel_____

Pink is the navy blue of India.

—Diana Vreeland

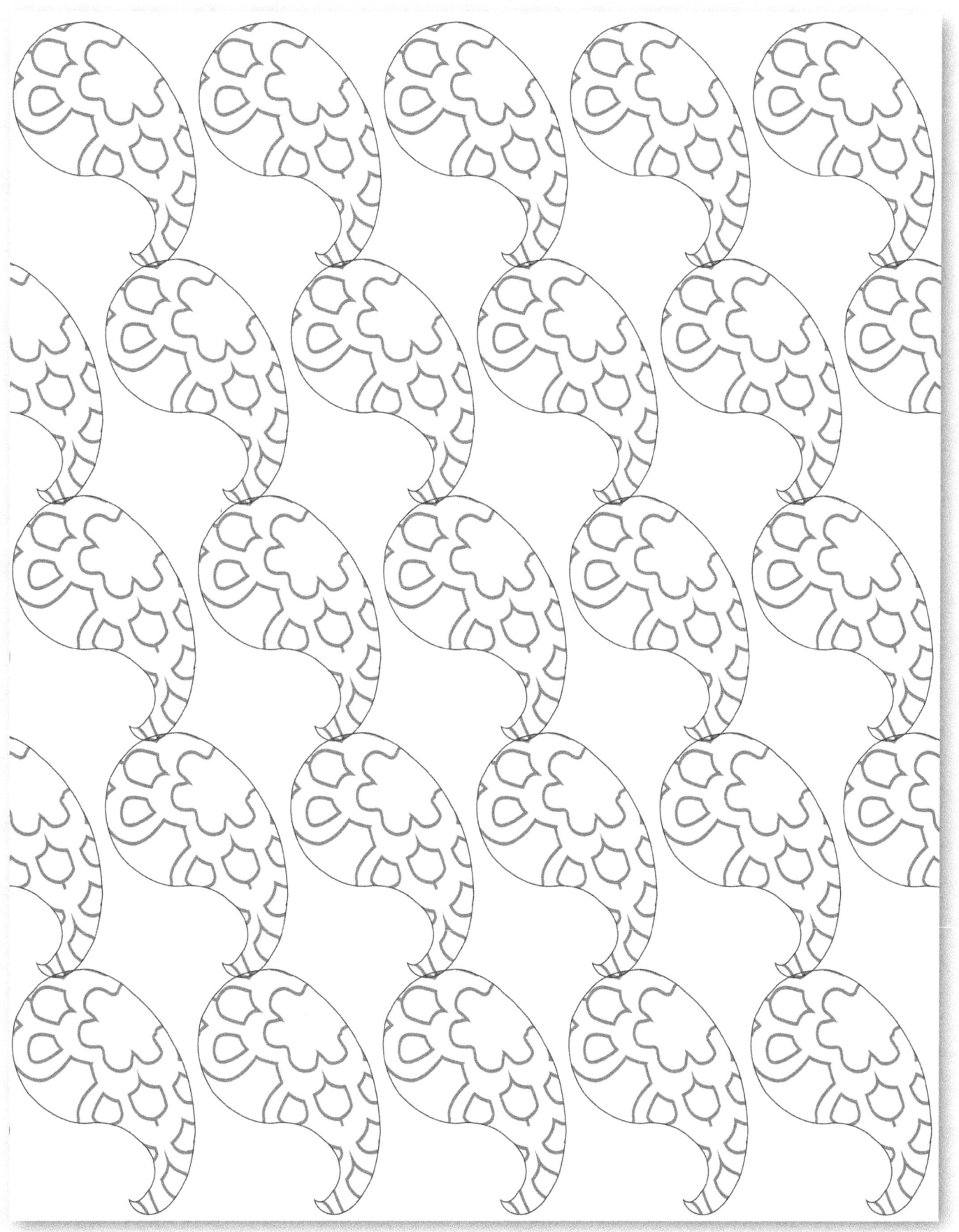

Barbara Jacobs

Your Notes and Drawings

Color Journal Page

This page is a way for you to keep track of any favorite colors or color "blends."
Enjoy using this extra space for your own drawings, notes, or stories.
Feel free to use the spaces for actual colors, not just words.

<u>Love this color</u>   <u>Mixed with this color</u>   <u>Result is this color</u>

Used on this page_____

Used these materials_____

What I love about this color or combination of colors_____

Makes me feel_____

It's all one to me: opera, painting,
drawing, faxes.

—David Hockney

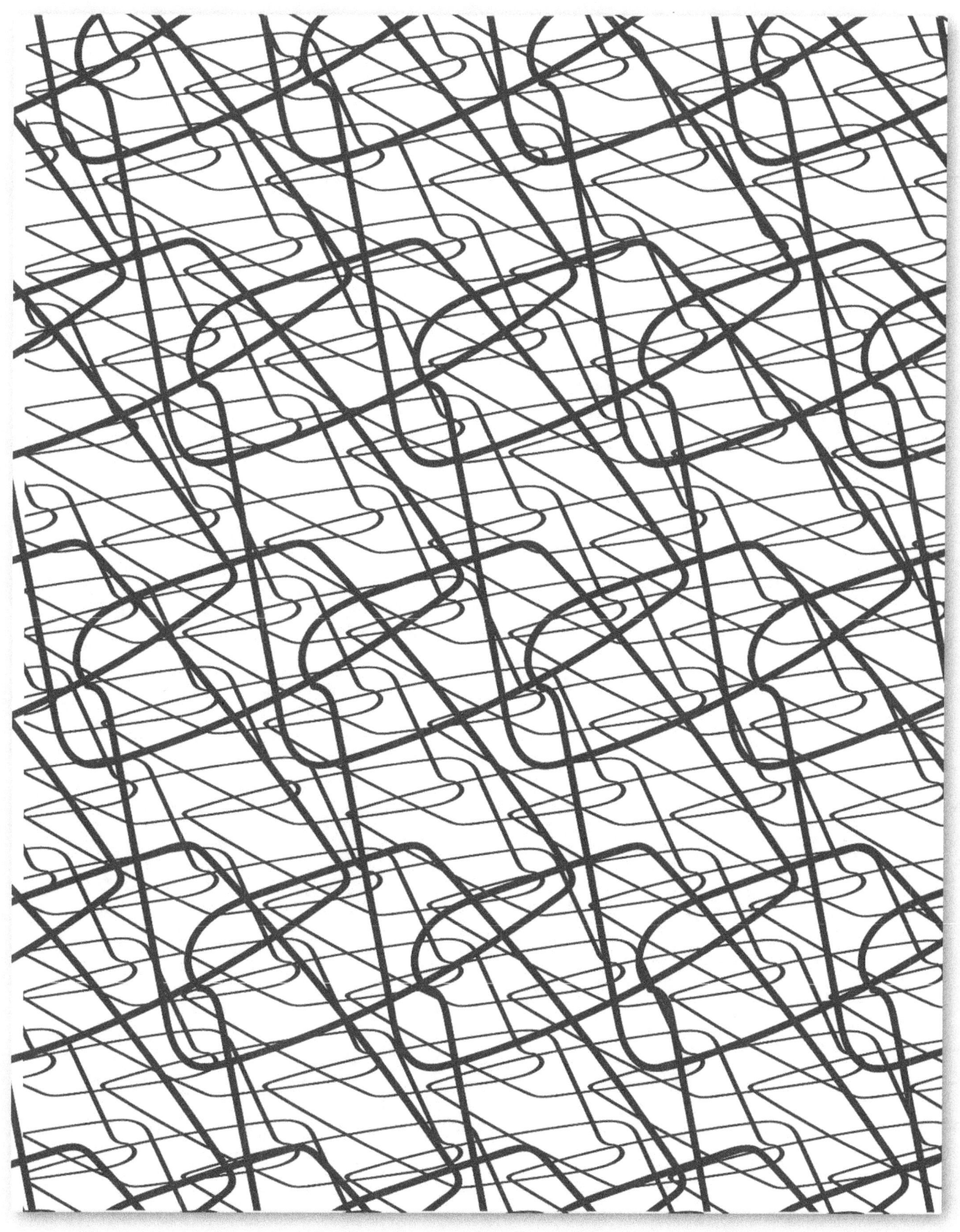

Barbara Jacobs

Your Notes and Drawings

Color Journal Page

This page is a way for you to keep track of any favorite colors or color "blends."
Enjoy using this extra space for your own drawings, notes, or stories.
Feel free to use the spaces for actual colors, not just words.

<u>Love this color</u>   <u>Mixed with this color</u>   <u>Result is this color</u>

Used on this page_____

Used these materials_____

What I love about this color or combination of colors_____

Makes me feel_____

The less effort, the more powerful and faster you will be.

— **Bruce Lee**

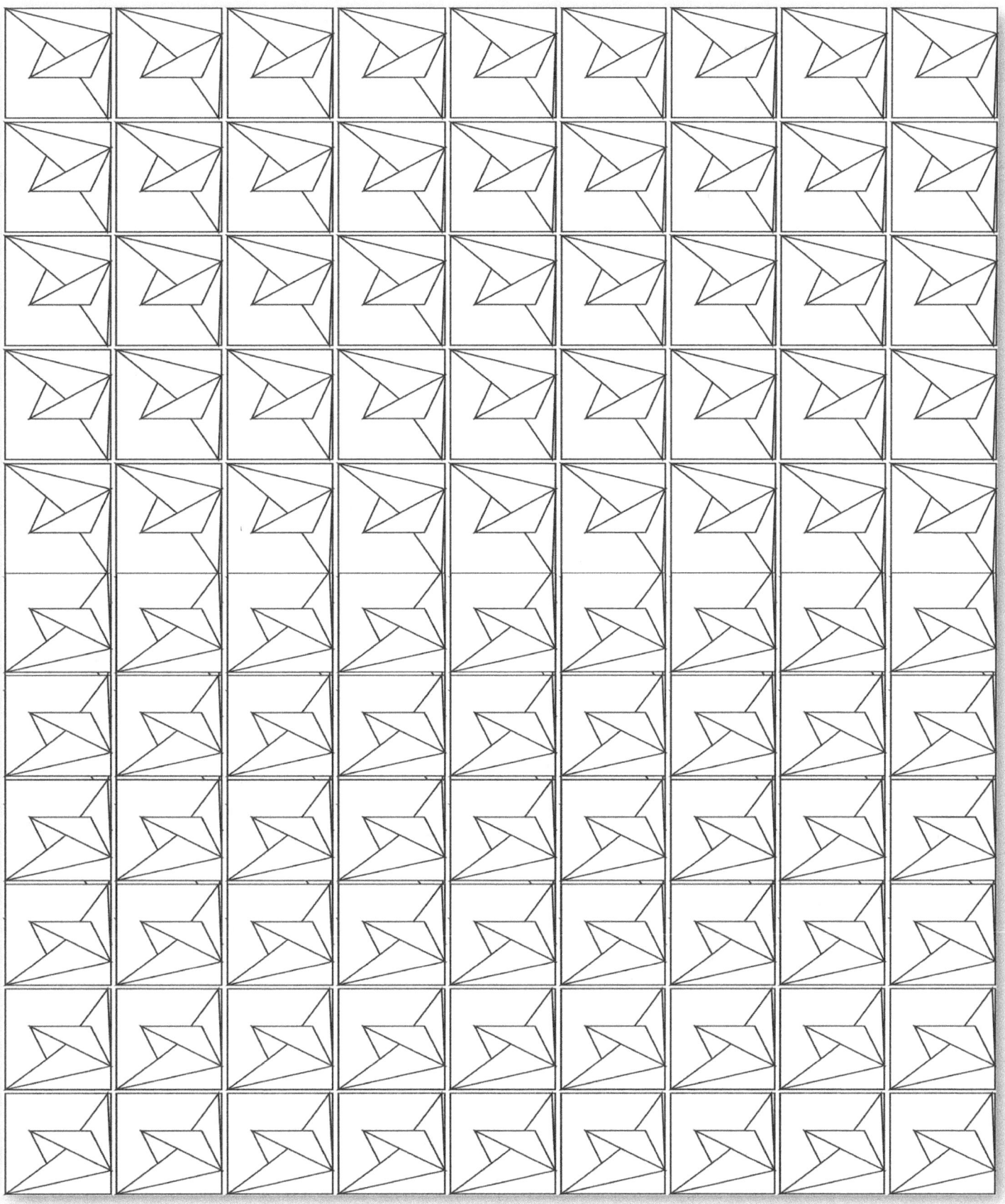

Barbara Jacobs

Your Notes and Drawings

Color Journal Page

This page is a way for you to keep track of any favorite colors or color "blends."
Enjoy using this extra space for your own drawings, notes, or stories.
Feel free to use the spaces for actual colors, not just words.

<u>Love this color</u>   <u>Mixed with this color</u>   <u>Result is this color</u>

Used on this page_____

Used these materials_____

What I love about this color or combination of colors_____

Makes me feel_____

Barbara Jacobs

Logic will get you from A to B.
Imagination will take you everywhere.

—Albert Einstein

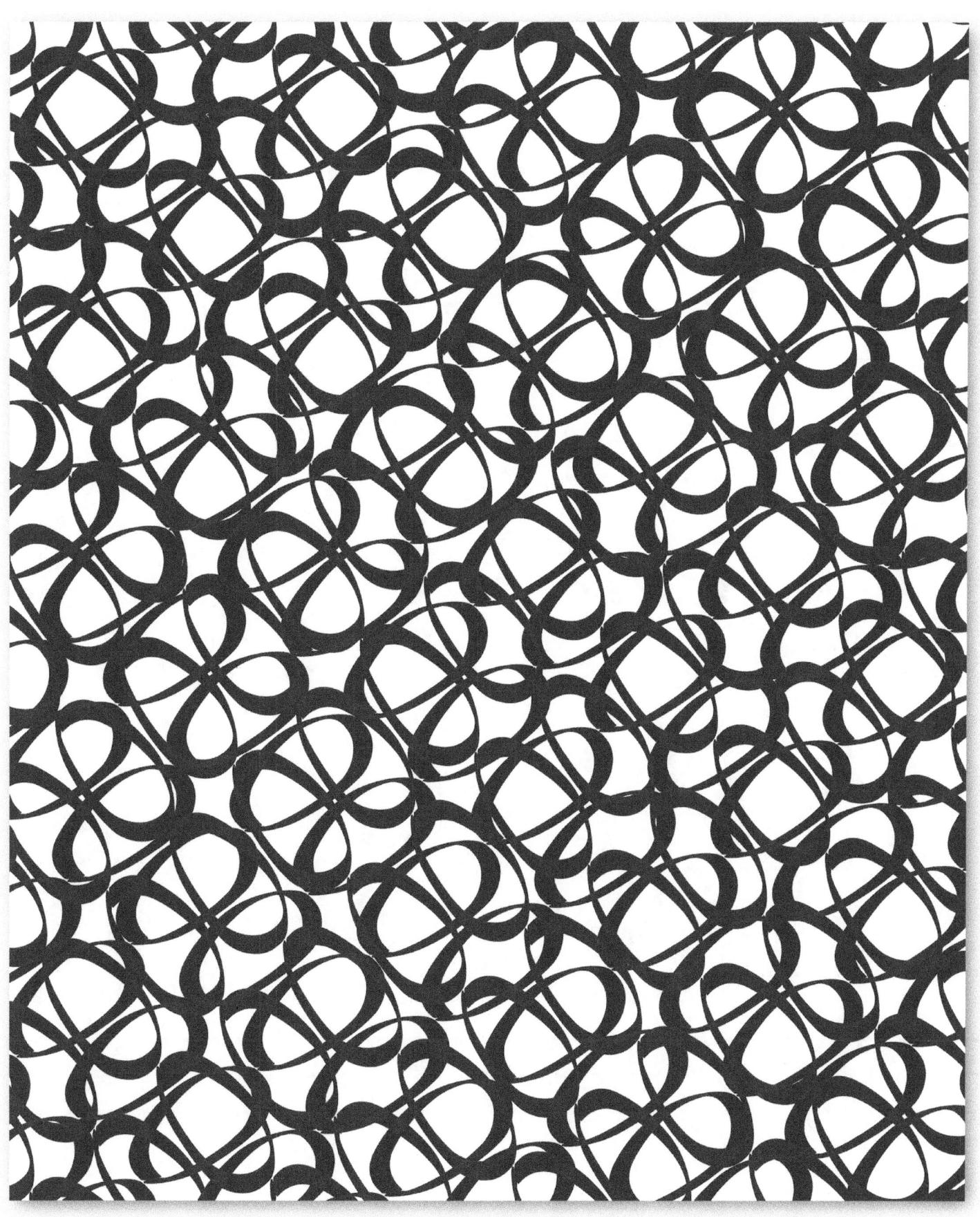

Barbara Jacobs

Your Notes and Drawings

Color Journal Page

This page is a way for you to keep track of any favorite colors or color "blends."
Enjoy using this extra space for your own drawings, notes, or stories.
Feel free to use the spaces for actual colors, not just words.

Love this color	Mixed with this color	Result is this color

Used on this page_____

Used these materials_____

What I love about this color or combination of colors_____

Makes me feel_____

The infinite is a square without corners.

—Chinese Proverb

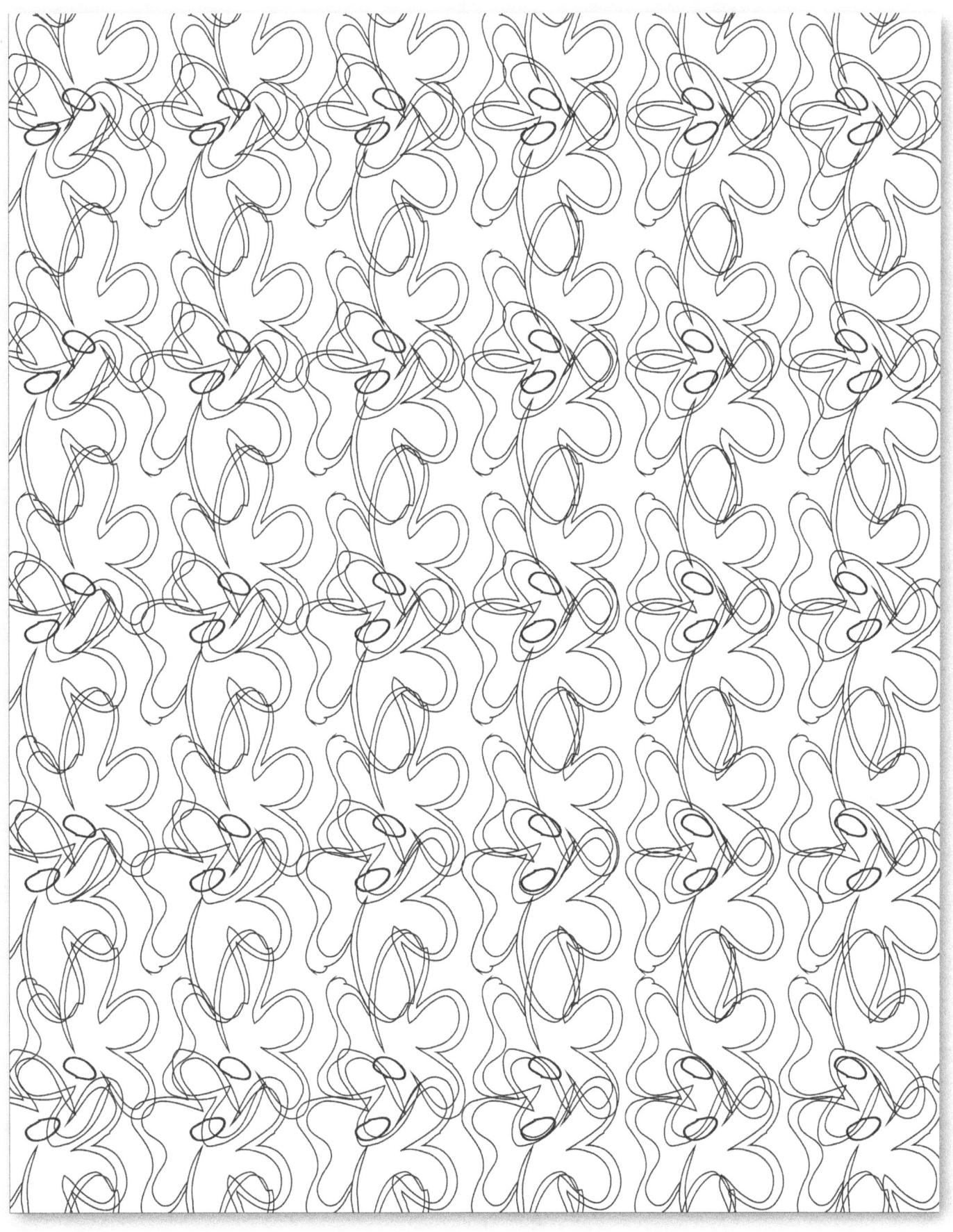

Barbara Jacobs

Your Notes and Drawings

Color Journal Page

This page is a way for you to keep track of any favorite colors or color "blends."
Enjoy using this extra space for your own drawings, notes, or stories.
Feel free to use the spaces for actual colors, not just words.

<u>Love this color</u>   <u>Mixed with this color</u>   <u>Result is this color</u>

Used on this page_____

Used these materials_____

What I love about this color or combination of colors_____

Makes me feel_____

A work of art is above all an adventure of the mind.

—Eugene Ionesco

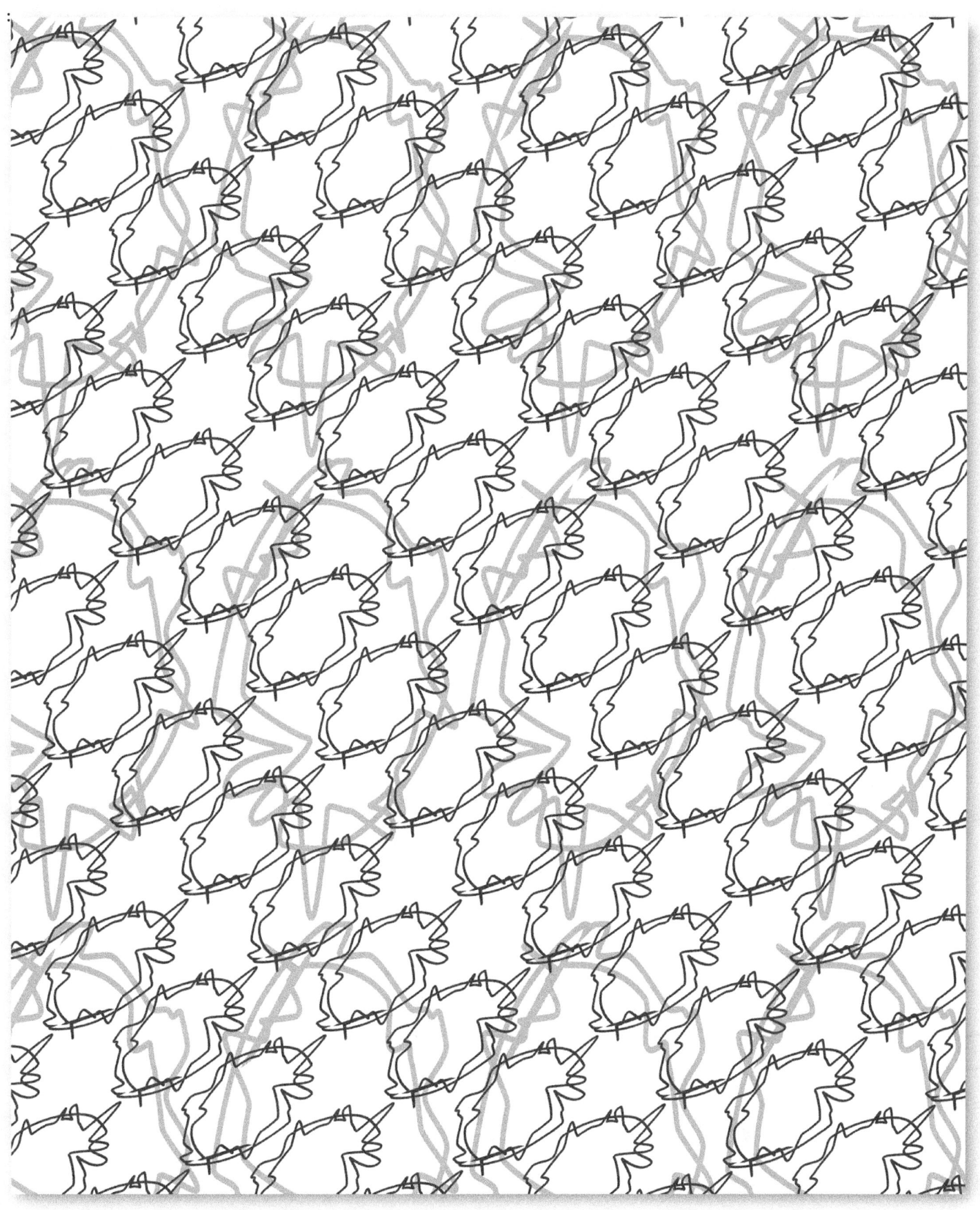

Barbara Jacobs

Your Notes and Drawings

Color Journal Page

This page is a way for you to keep track of any favorite colors or color "blends."
Enjoy using this extra space for your own drawings, notes, or stories.
Feel free to use the spaces for actual colors, not just words.

<u>Love this color</u>   <u>Mixed with this color</u>   <u>Result is this color</u>

Used on this page_____

Used these materials_____

What I love about this color or combination of colors_____

Makes me feel_____

Limit gives form to the limitless.

—Pythagoras

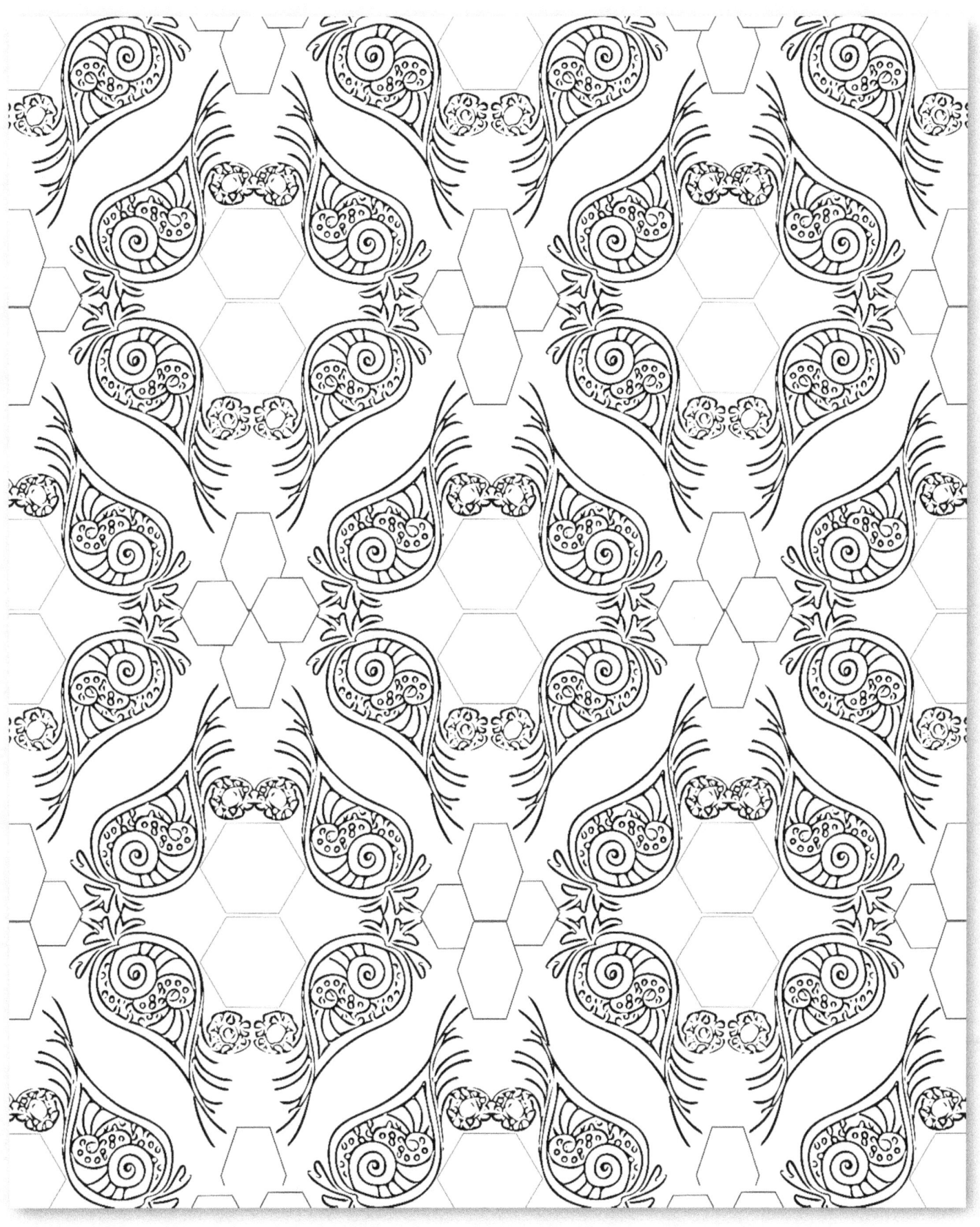

Barbara Jacobs

Your Notes and Drawings

Color Journal Page

This page is a way for you to keep track of any favorite colors or color "blends."
Enjoy using this extra space for your own drawings, notes, or stories.
Feel free to use the spaces for actual colors, not just words.

<u>Love this color</u>   <u>Mixed with this color</u>   <u>Result is this color</u>

Used on this page_____

Used these materials_____

What I love about this color or combination of colors_____

Makes me feel_____

Barbara Jacobs

*It's better to make a creative mistake than
a stagnant work in good taste.*

—Phillipe Starck

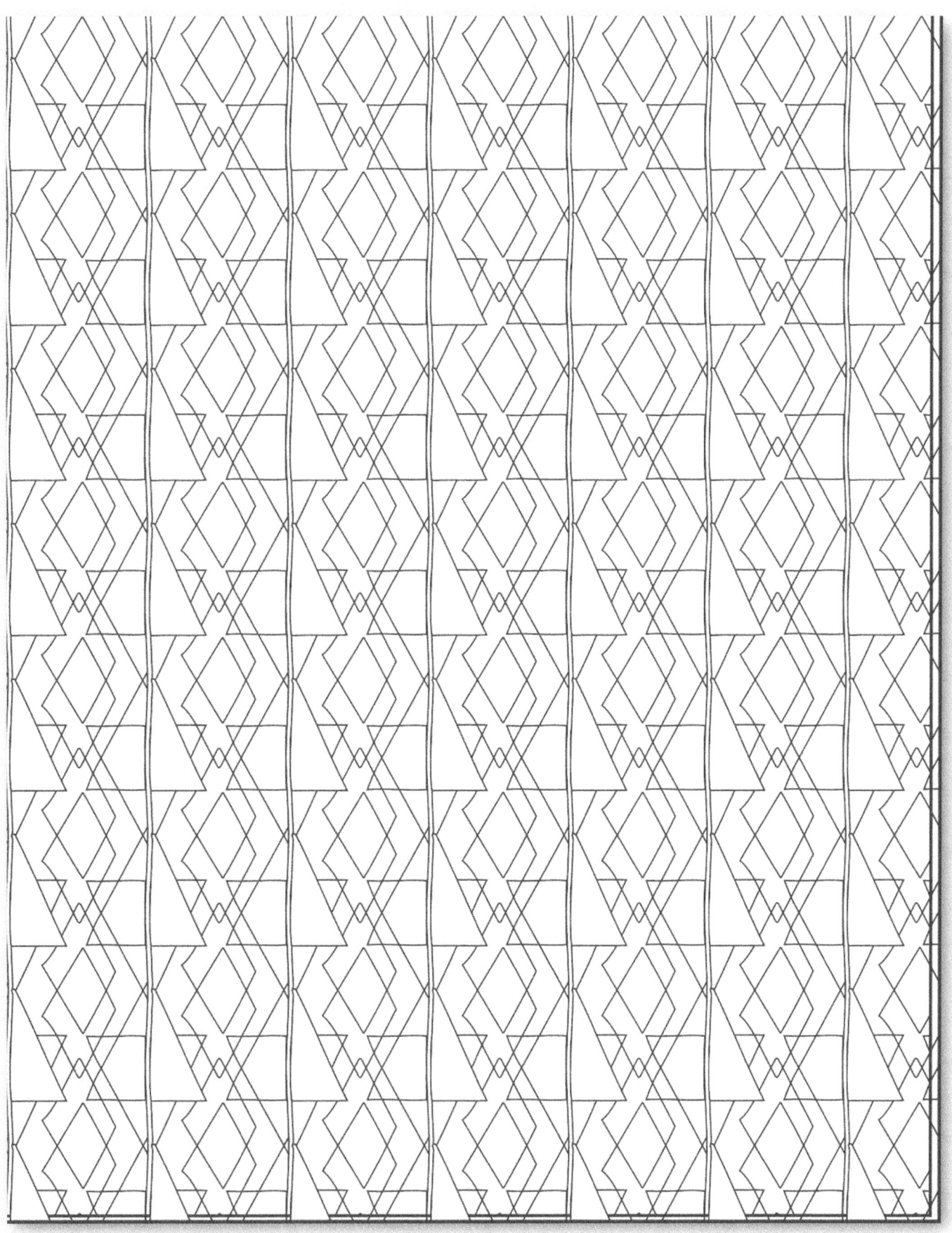

Barbara Jacobs

Your Notes and Drawings

Color Journal Page

This page is a way for you to keep track of any favorite colors or color "blends."
Enjoy using this extra space for your own drawings, notes, or stories.
Feel free to use the spaces for actual colors, not just words.

<u>Love this color</u>   <u>Mixed with this color</u>   <u>Result is this color</u>

Used on this page_____

Used these materials_____

What I love about this color or combination of colors_____

Makes me feel_____

*Nothing is impossible, the word itself says
'I'm possible!'*

—Audrey Hepburn

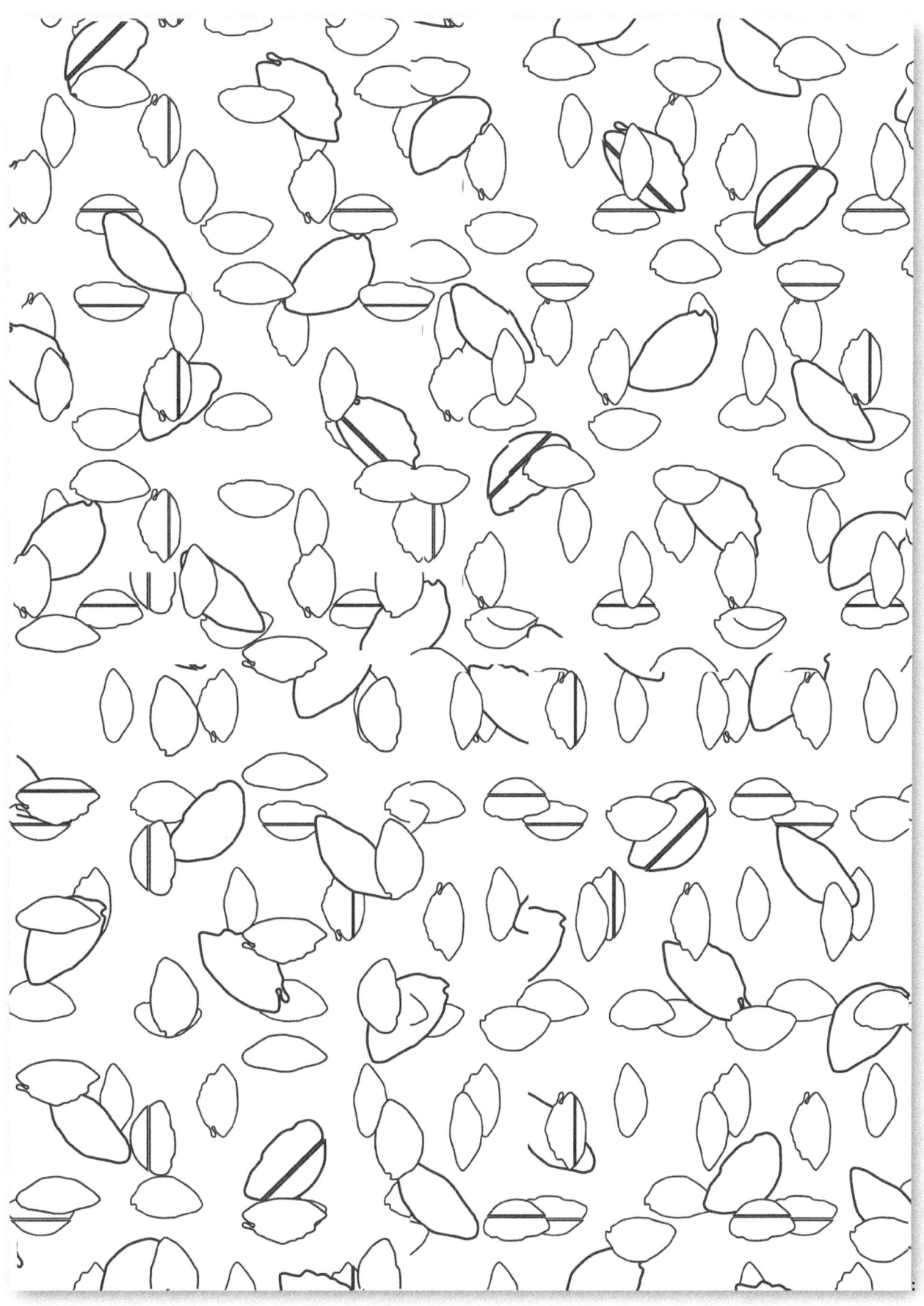

Barbara Jacobs

Your Notes and Drawings

Color Journal Page

This page is a way for you to keep track of any favorite colors or color "blends."
Enjoy using this extra space for your own drawings, notes, or stories.
Feel free to use the spaces for actual colors, not just words.

<u>Love this color</u>   <u>Mixed with this color</u>   <u>Result is this color</u>

Used on this page_____

Used these materials_____

What I love about this color or combination of colors_____

Makes me feel_____

To gaze is to think.

—Salvador Dali

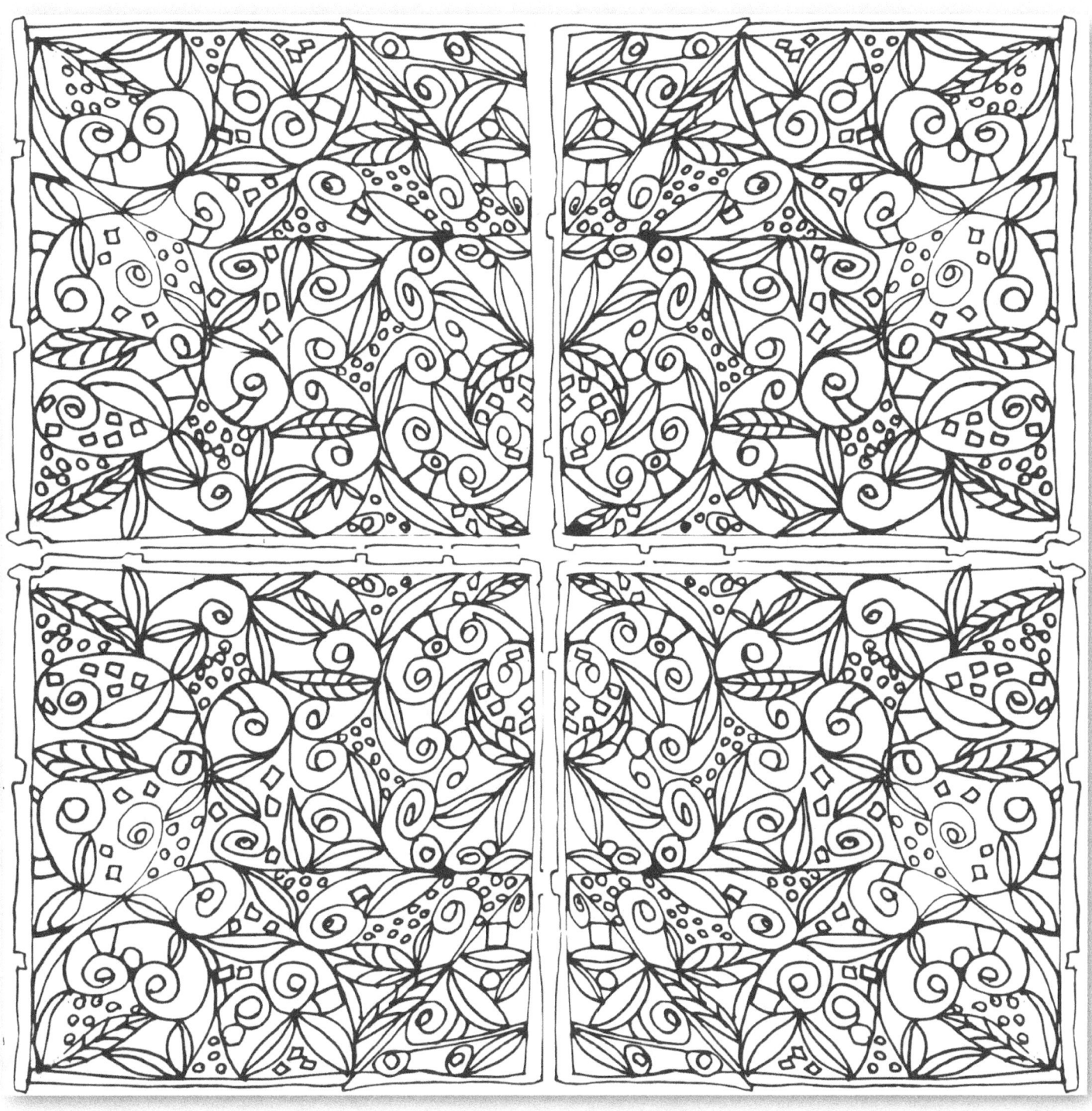

Barbara Jacobs

Your Notes and Drawings

Color Journal Page

This page is a way for you to keep track of any favorite colors or color "blends."
Enjoy using this extra space for your own drawings, notes, or stories.
Feel free to use the spaces for actual colors, not just words.

Love this color	Mixed with this color	Result is this color

Used on this page_____

Used these materials_____

What I love about this color or combination of colors_____

Makes me feel_____

Barbara Jacobs

I believe a leaf of grass is no less than
the journey-work of the stars.

—Walt Whitman

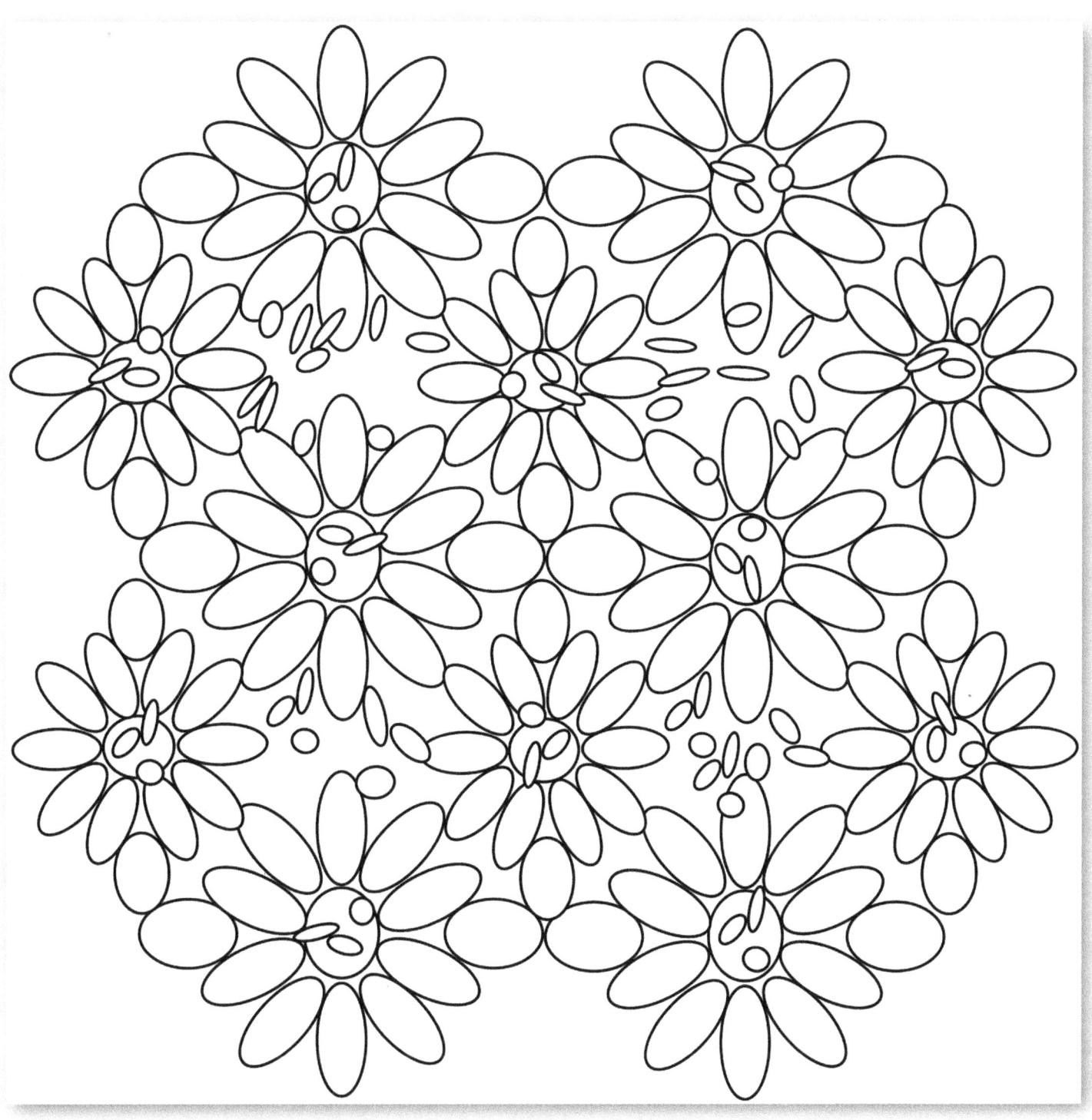

Barbara Jacobs

Your Notes and Drawings

Color Journal Page

This page is a way for you to keep track of any favorite colors or color "blends."
Enjoy using this extra space for your own drawings, notes, or stories.
Feel free to use the spaces for actual colors, not just words.

<u>Love this color</u>   <u>Mixed with this color</u>   <u>Result is this color</u>

Used on this page_____

Used these materials_____

What I love about this color or combination of colors_____

Makes me feel_____

Barbara Jacobs

Give me a laundry list and I will set it to music.

—Giacomo Puccini

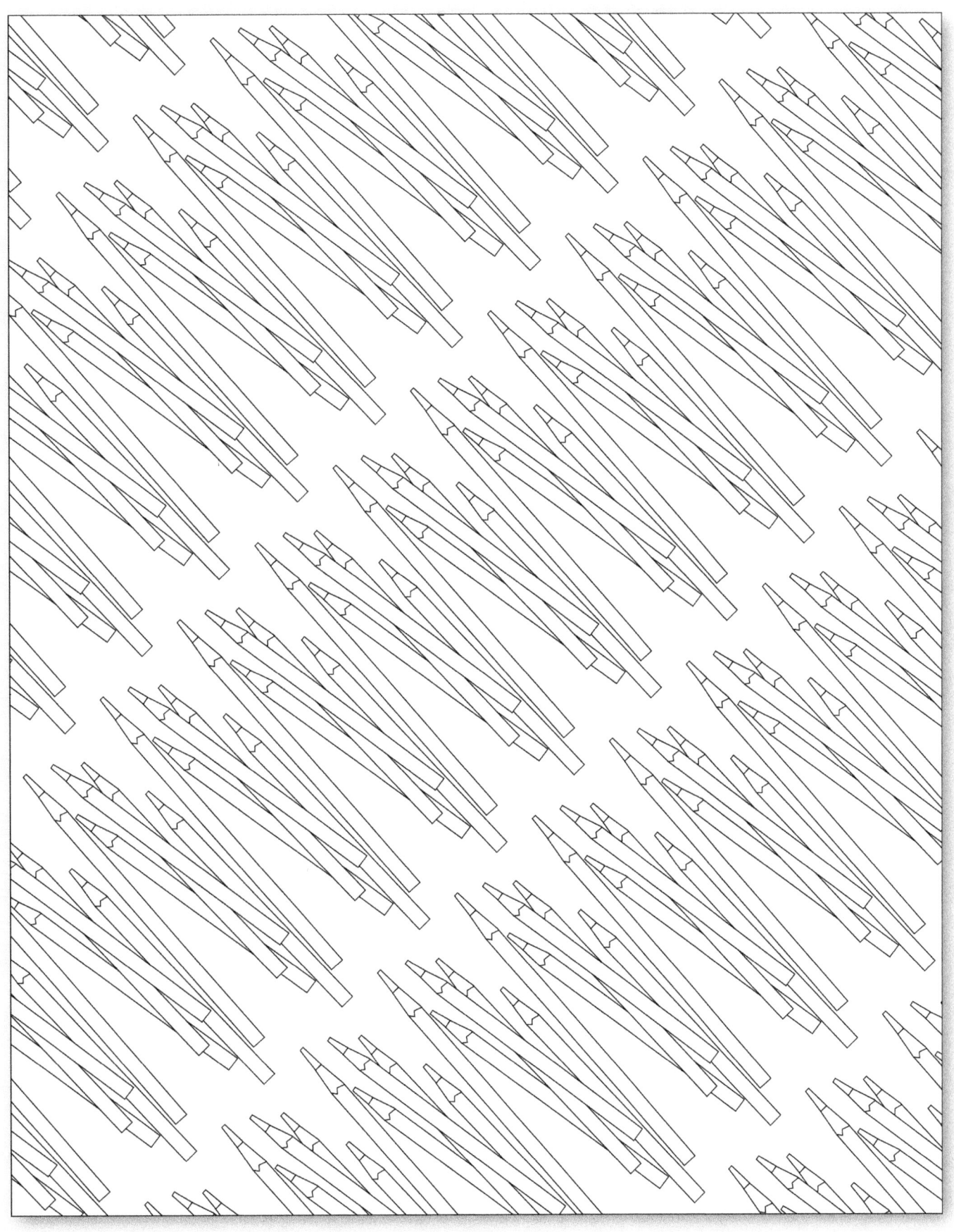

Barbara Jacobs

Your Notes and Drawings

Color Journal Page

This page is a way for you to keep track of any favorite colors or color "blends."
Enjoy using this extra space for your own drawings, notes, or stories.
Feel free to use the spaces for actual colors, not just words.

Love this color	Mixed with this color	Result is this color

Used on this page_____

Used these materials_____

What I love about this color or combination of colors_____

Makes me feel_____

Jumping from boulder to boulder and never falling, with a heavy pack, is easier than it sounds; you just can't fall when you get into the rhythm of the dance.

—Jack Kerouac, *The Dharma Bums*

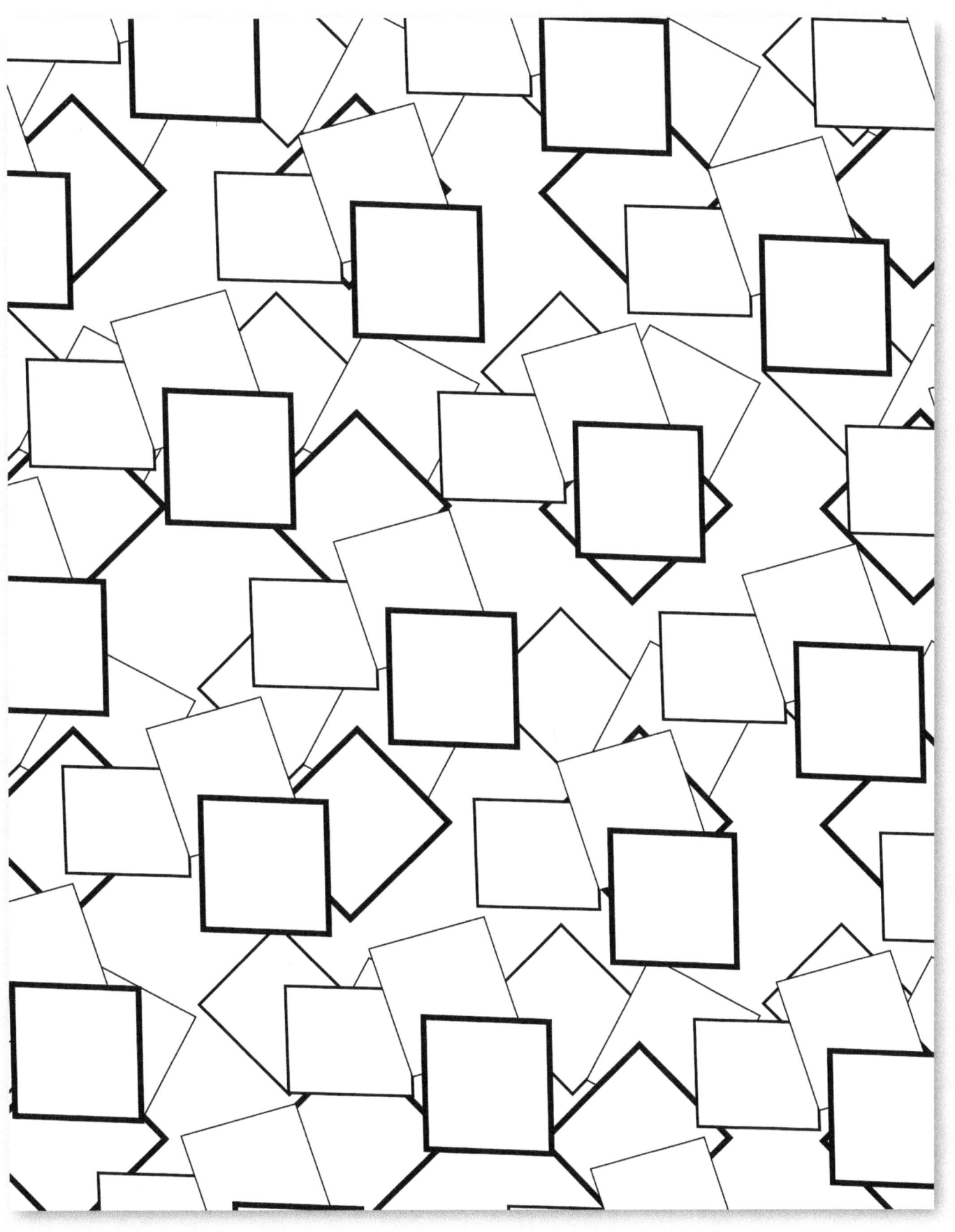

Barbara Jacobs

Your Notes and Drawings

Color Journal Page

This page is a way for you to keep track of any favorite colors or color "blends."
Enjoy using this extra space for your own drawings, notes, or stories.
Feel free to use the spaces for actual colors, not just words.

<u>Love this color</u>   <u>**Mixed with this color**</u>   <u>**Result is this color**</u>

Used on this page_____

Used these materials_____

What I love about this color or combination of colors_____

Makes me feel_____

Barbara Jacobs

We look at the present through a rear-view mirror…we march backwards into the future.

—Marshall McLuhan

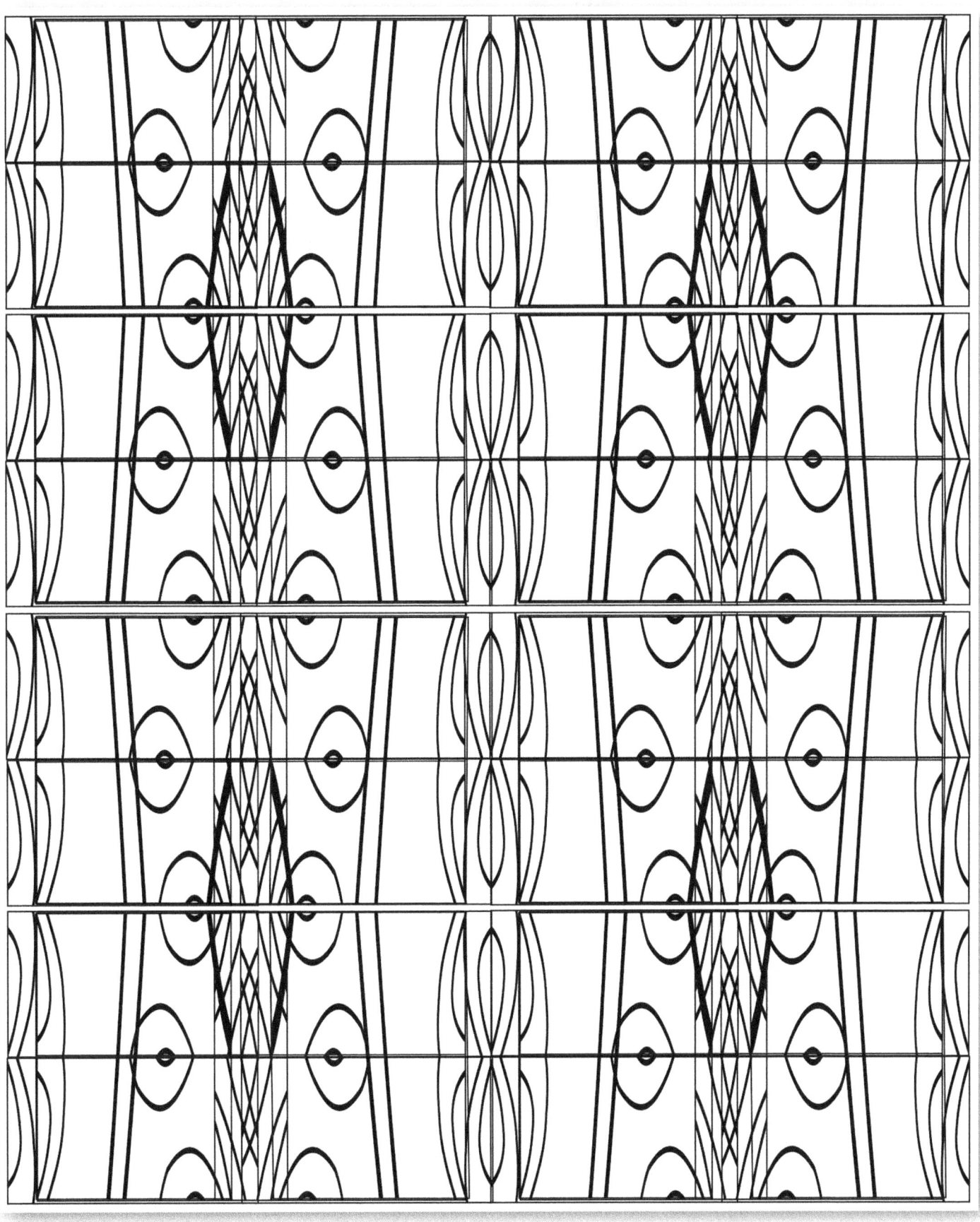

Barbara Jacobs

Your Notes and Drawings

Color Journal Page

This page is a way for you to keep track of any favorite colors or color "blends."
Enjoy using this extra space for your own drawings, notes, or stories.
Feel free to use the spaces for actual colors, not just words.

Love this color	Mixed with this color	Result is this color

Used on this page_____

Used these materials_____

What I love about this color or combination of colors_____

Makes me feel_____

Barbara Jacobs

I was walking along
minding my business
When love came and hit me in the eye
(Flash, bam, alakazam)
Out of an orange colored sky

—Nat "King" Cole

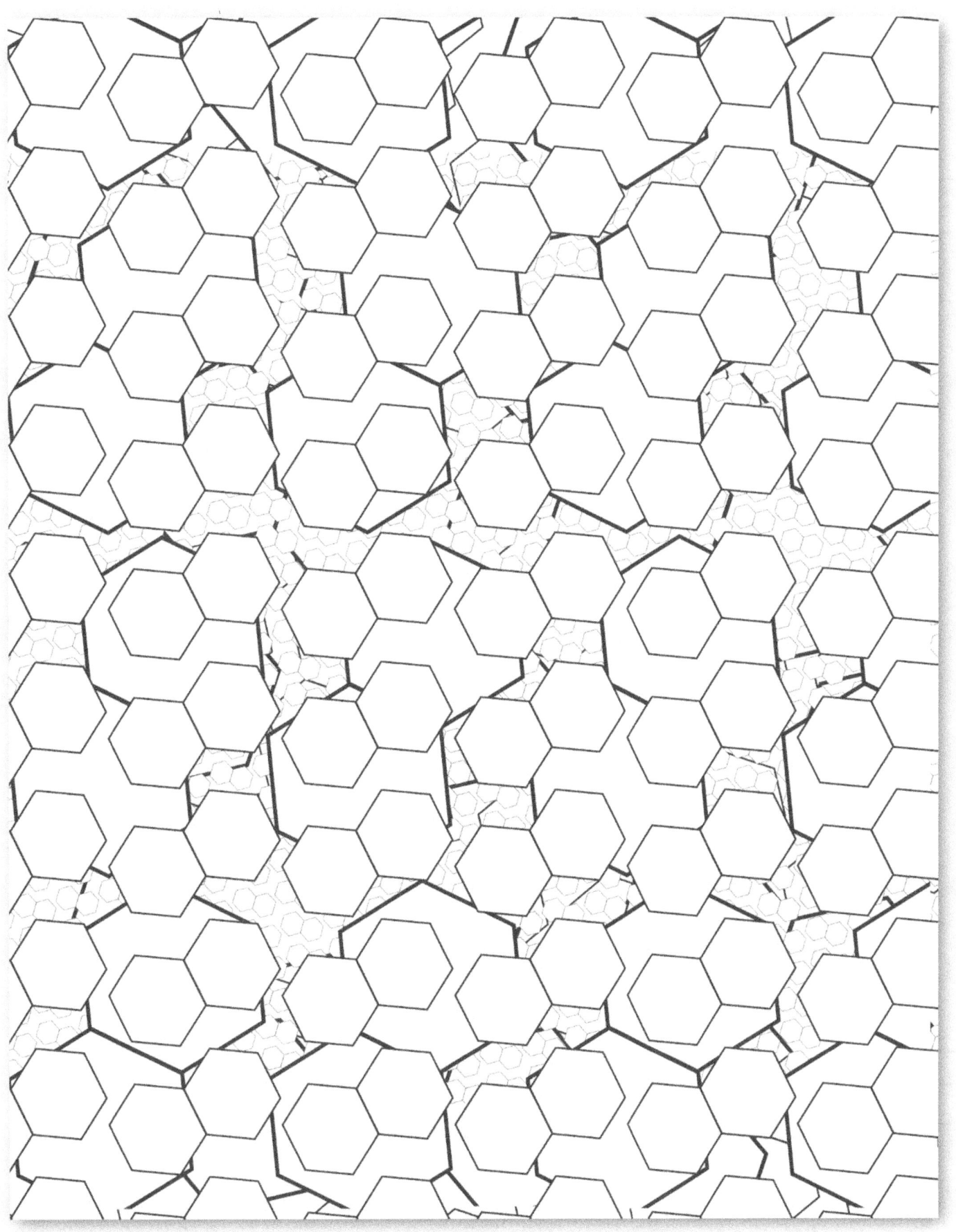

Barbara Jacobs

Your Notes and Drawings

Color Journal Page

This page is a way for you to keep track of any favorite colors or color "blends."
Enjoy using this extra space for your own drawings, notes, or stories.
Feel free to use the spaces for actual colors, not just words.

<u>Love this color</u>   <u>Mixed with this color</u>   <u>Result is this color</u>

Used on this page_____

Used these materials_____

What I love about this color or combination of colors_____

Makes me feel_____

Barbara Jacobs

Your Notes and Drawings

Your Notes and Drawings

Color Journal Page

This page is a way for you to keep track of any favorite colors or color "blends."
Enjoy using this extra space for your own drawings, notes, or stories.
Feel free to use the spaces for actual colors, not just words.

<u>Love this color</u>   <u>Mixed with this color</u>   <u>Result is this color</u>

Used on this page_____

Used these materials_____

What I love about this color or combination of colors_____

Makes me feel_____

Barbara Jacobs

We don't see things as they are,
we see them as we are.

—Anais Nin

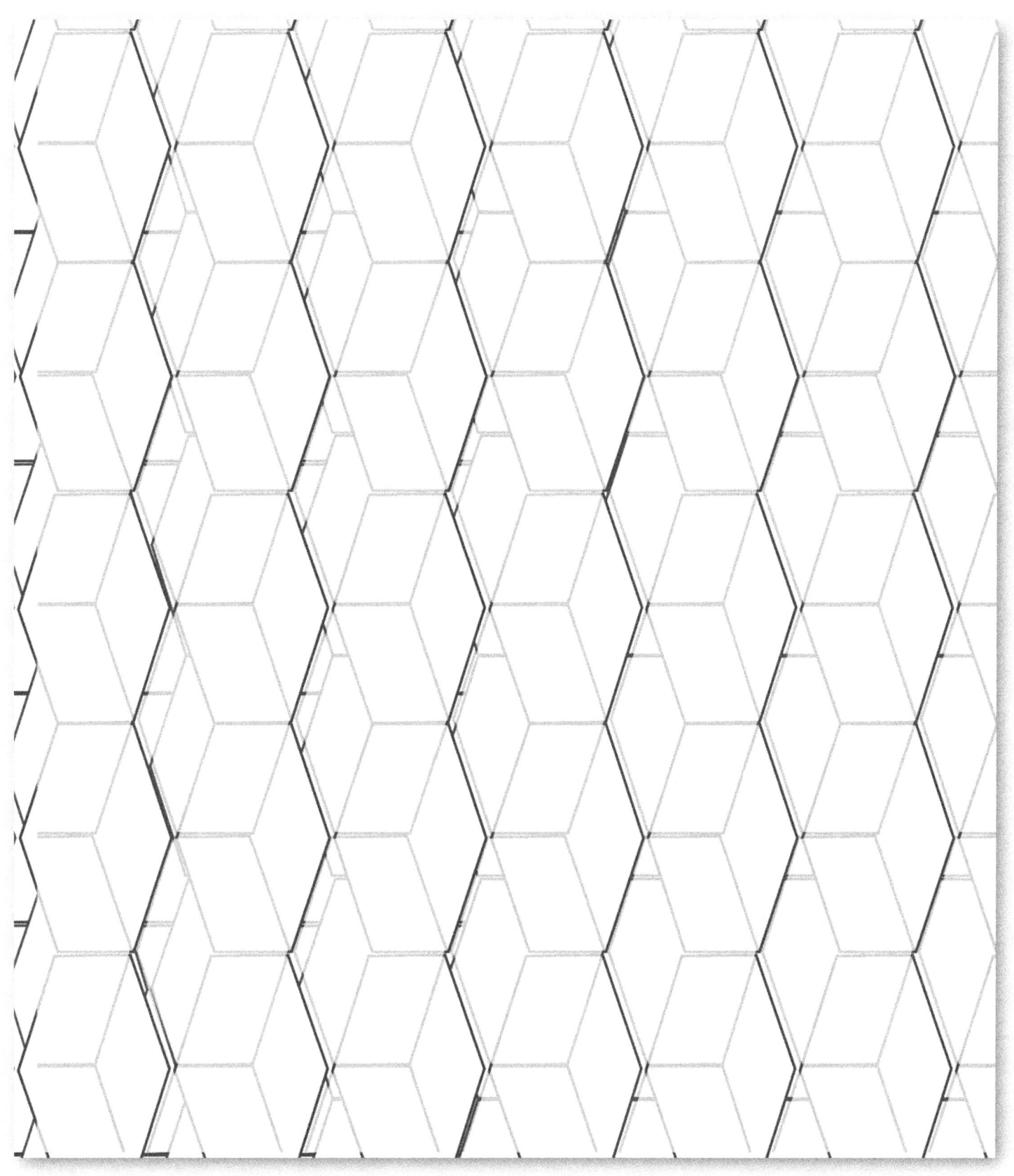

Barbara Jacobs

Your Notes and Drawings

Color Journal Page

This page is a way for you to keep track of any favorite colors or color "blends."
Enjoy using this extra space for your own drawings, notes, or stories.
Feel free to use the spaces for actual colors, not just words.

Love this color	Mixed with this color	Result is this color

Used on this page_____

Used these materials_____

What I love about this color or combination of colors_____

Makes me feel_____

Barbara Jacobs

*Isn't life a series of images that change
as they repeat themselves?*

—Andy Warhol

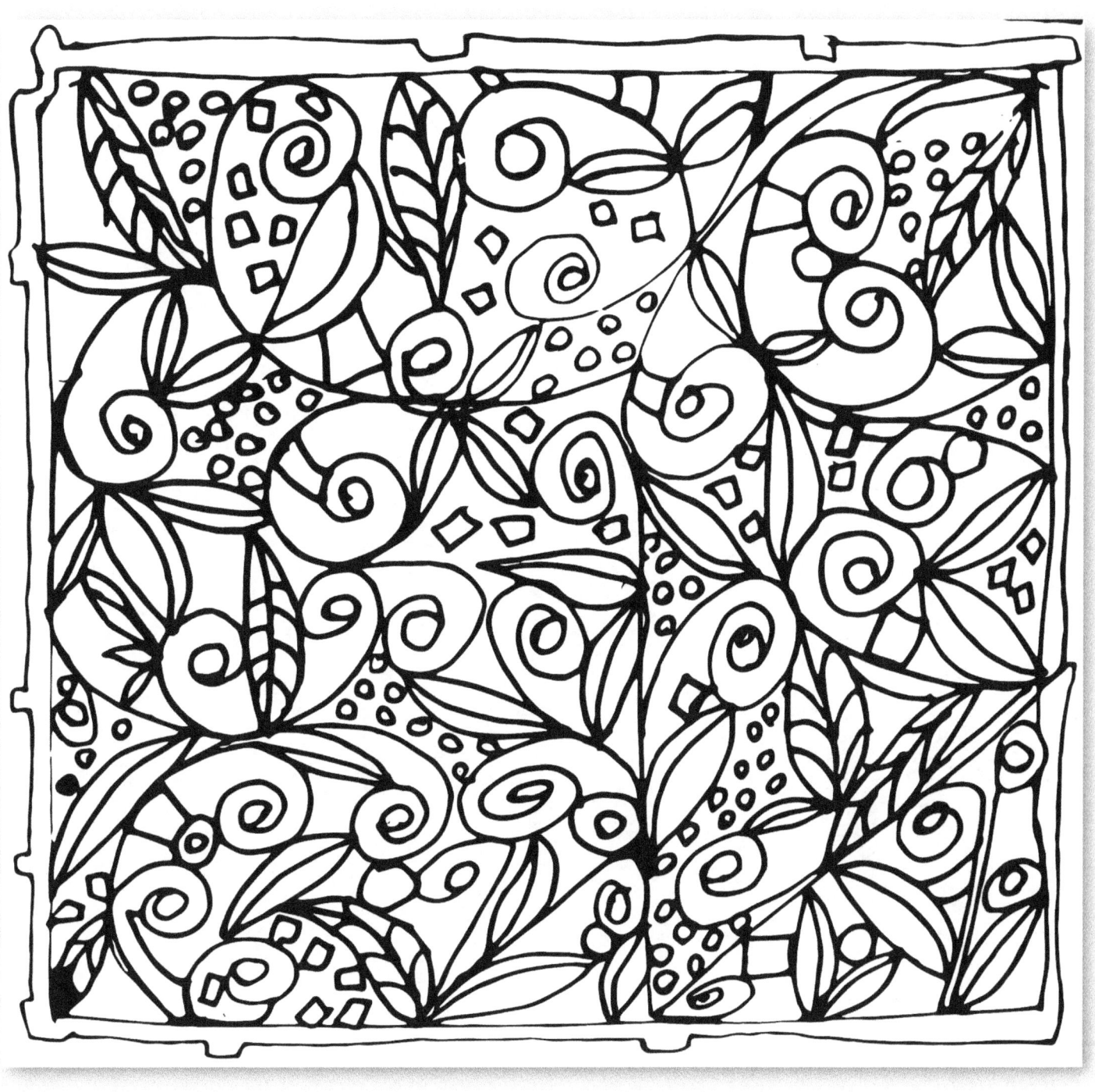

Barbara Jacobs

Your Notes and Drawings

Color Journal Page

This page is a way for you to keep track of any favorite colors or color "blends."
Enjoy using this extra space for your own drawings, notes, or stories.
Feel free to use the spaces for actual colors, not just words.

<u>Love this color</u>   <u>Mixed with this color</u>   <u>Result is this color</u>

Used on this page_____

Used these materials_____

What I love about this color or combination of colors_____

Makes me feel_____

I would venture to warn against too great intimacy with artists as it is very seductive and a little dangerous.

—Queen Victoria

A Color Associations Quiz - Here are your answers!

Now that you've had a chance to try your hand at interpreting these descriptions, see the 'answers' below. As with any subject worth considering seriously, this is just the tip of the iceberg. Some may be familiar, others might surprise you. In any case, enjoy!

Some descriptions will apply to more than one color.

- Casual and youthful; Stimulates and suggests a sour taste: *Yellow, Chartreuse*
- Favorite color of young girls: *Lavender, Pink*
- Can induce a rise in blood pressure: *Gray, Red*
- Stimulates and suggests a sweet smell: *Pink*
- Friendly and casual; sometimes associated with poison: *Chartreuse*
- Empowers, stimulates, increases appetite symbolizes passion, creates drama: *Red*
- Compliant; suggests intimacy and affection: *Pink*
- Promotes informality, activity; cheers, expands, implies "affordable": *Orange*
- Expands, warms, welcomes, cheers; promotes communication, anticipation; implies newness or something temporary: *Yellow*
- Balances, refreshes; creates a resting place; can be showy and dynamic: *Green*
- Relaxes, refreshes and cools; supports tranquility, trust and peace; symbolizes knowledge, integrity, respect, and quality: *Blue*
- Aristocratic; creates mystery; inspires imagination and intuition: *Purple / Deep Violet*
- Symbolizes stability and security; friendly and receptive: *Brown*
- Purifies, lights, expands, cleans, unifies, enlivens other colors: *White*
- Symbolizes status, elegance and formality; conveys strength and authority; can be ominous: *Black*
- May cause occupants of the area to become inattentive, sleepy, or agitated: *White*
- Can imply emotional dependence: *Pink*
- Sometimes interpreted as a spiritual color: *Purple, Lavender, White*

This is just the beginning.
The associations and effects of color are modified when colors are used in combination.

—⋙—

About Barbara

Barbara's formal artistic education includes work done at the *Accademia di Belle Arti di Firenze* in Florence, Italy; the University of California, Berkeley, where she studied with Adja Yunkers and David Hockney; and the University of Minnesota, where she received her Bachelor of Arts in studio art with a concentration in painting and printmaking.

In addition to private commission work, Barbara enjoys participating in exhibitions whenever possible. While living in Massachusetts, from 1986 to 1990 she was awarded grants from the Massachusetts Council on the Arts to teach hands-on design seminars on the traditional design methods and decorative arts techniques of many cultures.

In 2000 she was awarded color design accreditation by the *IACC (International Association of Color Consultants/ Designe*rs), the subject of her thesis project being on the importance of color in the elementary school environment. Her work has been shown internationally through the *IACC*.

Barbara's programs on color and design have been enjoyed by audiences in various educational settings; grants to teach high school students, architects, and in professional organizations like *NeoCon* in Atlanta and Chicago. Her professional affiliations also have included *ASID (American Society of Interior Designers / Industry Partner)* and *CMG (Color Marketing Group)*. She has been published in a variety of professional and shelter media, both in print and online.

With her unique perspective as an artist, designer, and colorist, Barbara's vision and her interest in incorporating a variety of materials and textures result in mixed-media, two-and-three-dimensional art work and mixed-media fibers in the rug designs and print pattern designs that explore an eclectic range of color, space, texture, and emotional appeal. Both fine art and designs range from the "painterly" to more structured, sometimes including historic or inter-cultural design references or whimsical motifs.

Windows to Imagination is a combination of Barbara's color and design experience and her own artwork.